Ahuva Muzikansky – Painter & Sculptor

Published by: Yotzrim Art Gallery - Consulting and selling art
Design: Roni oz

© All rights reserved to Yotzrim Art Gallery - Consulting and Sale of Art- 2021
www.yotzrimgallery.com

Address: PO Box 5123, Herzliya, ZIP Code 4649719
Phone: +972-54-5286808

Do not reproduce, copy, photograph, record, translate, store in a database, transmit or receive in any way or transmit data from it in any form or electronic means, optical or mechanical or otherwise - any part of the material in this book. Commercial use of any kind of material contained in this book is strictly prohibited without the prior permission of the creators of the gallery.

Ahuva Muzikansky
Painter & Sculptor

Ahuva Muzikansky

multidisciplinary artist, painter, sculptor on a metal net and wire and jewelry designer. Studied painting with Edwin Salomon and sculpture with sculptor Sonia Natra. Most of the paintings are made on canvas, in acrylic paints with the help of scalys and paint spray almost brushless, sometimes combined with metal wires and old pieces of fabrics.

The subjects of the painting influenced by the events and daily life surrounds her, from abstract to human figures, especially women. The paintings are colourful and full of energy and emotion. Ahuva exhibited in galleries and participated in group exhibitions around the country

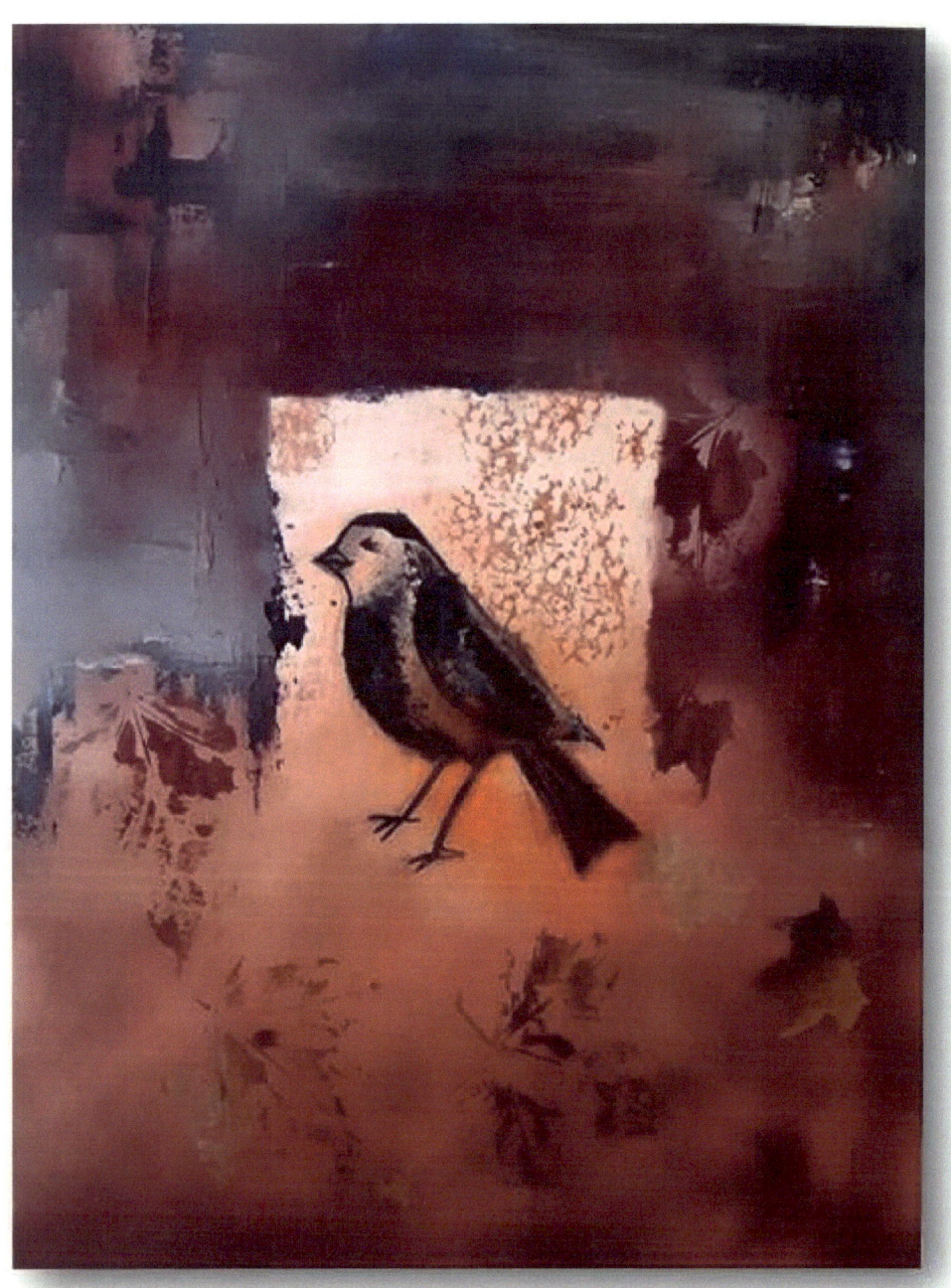
Acrylic on canvas, 90 by 70 cm

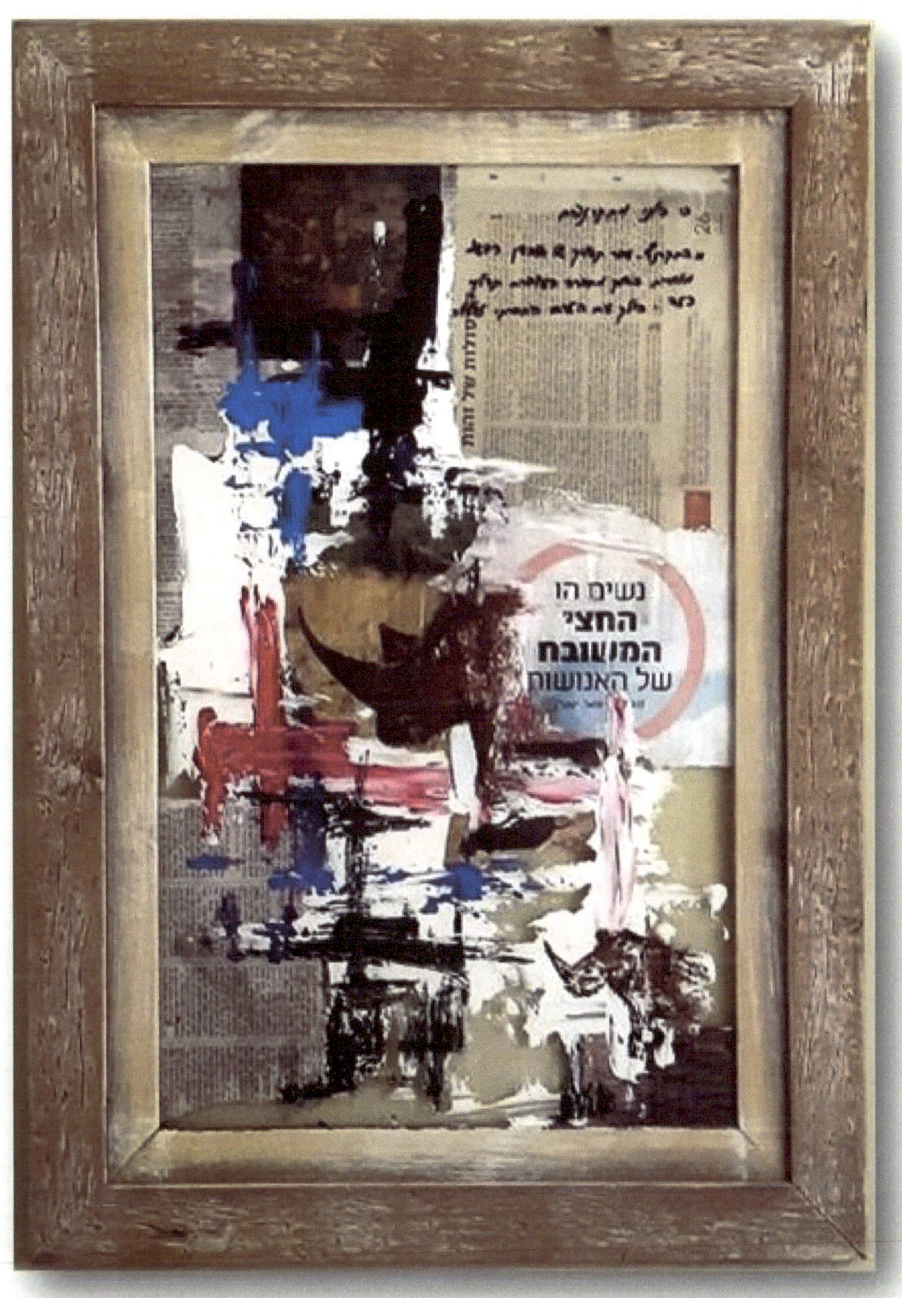

Mix Media Acrylic on glass, 88 by 62 cm

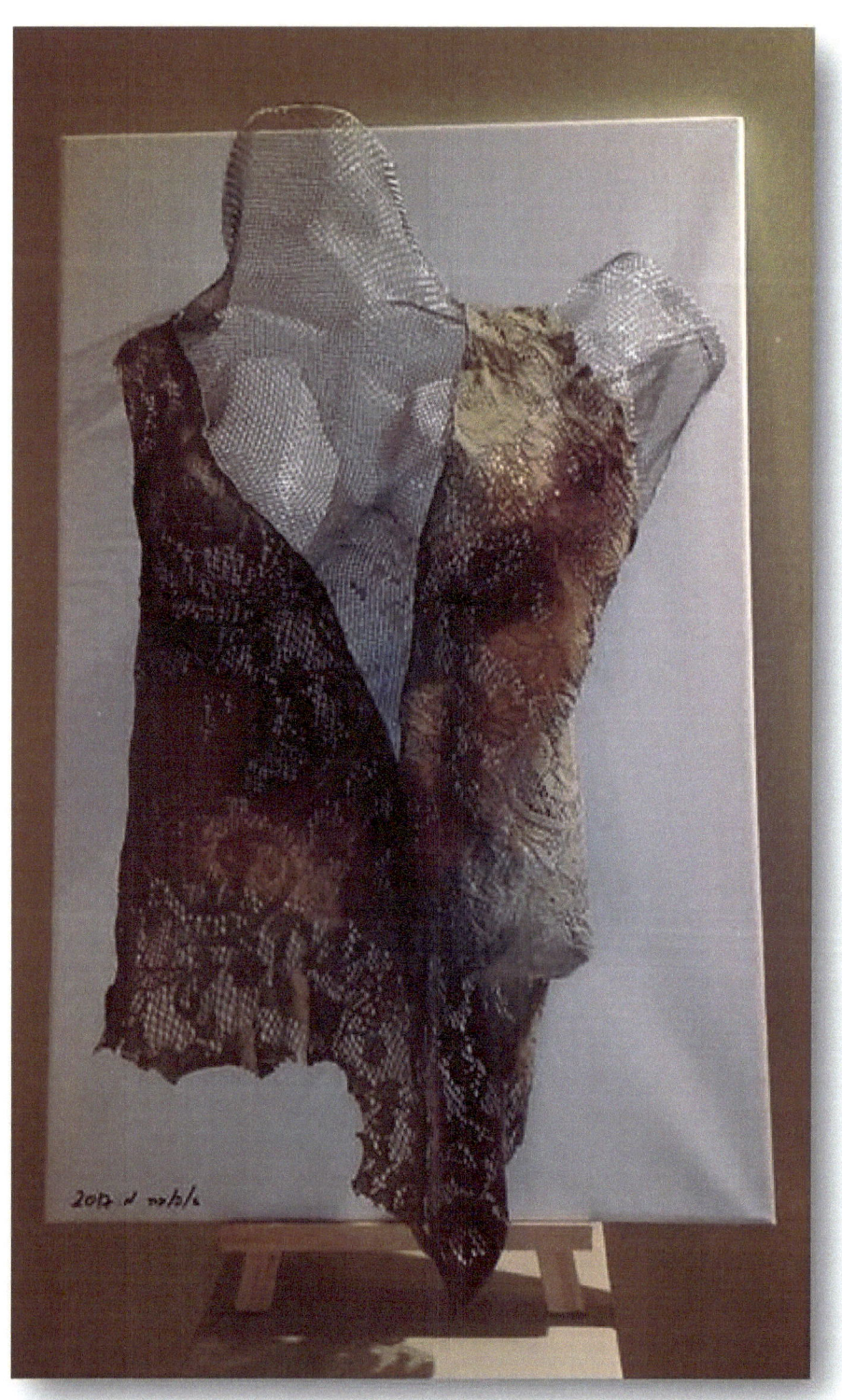

Grid sculpture

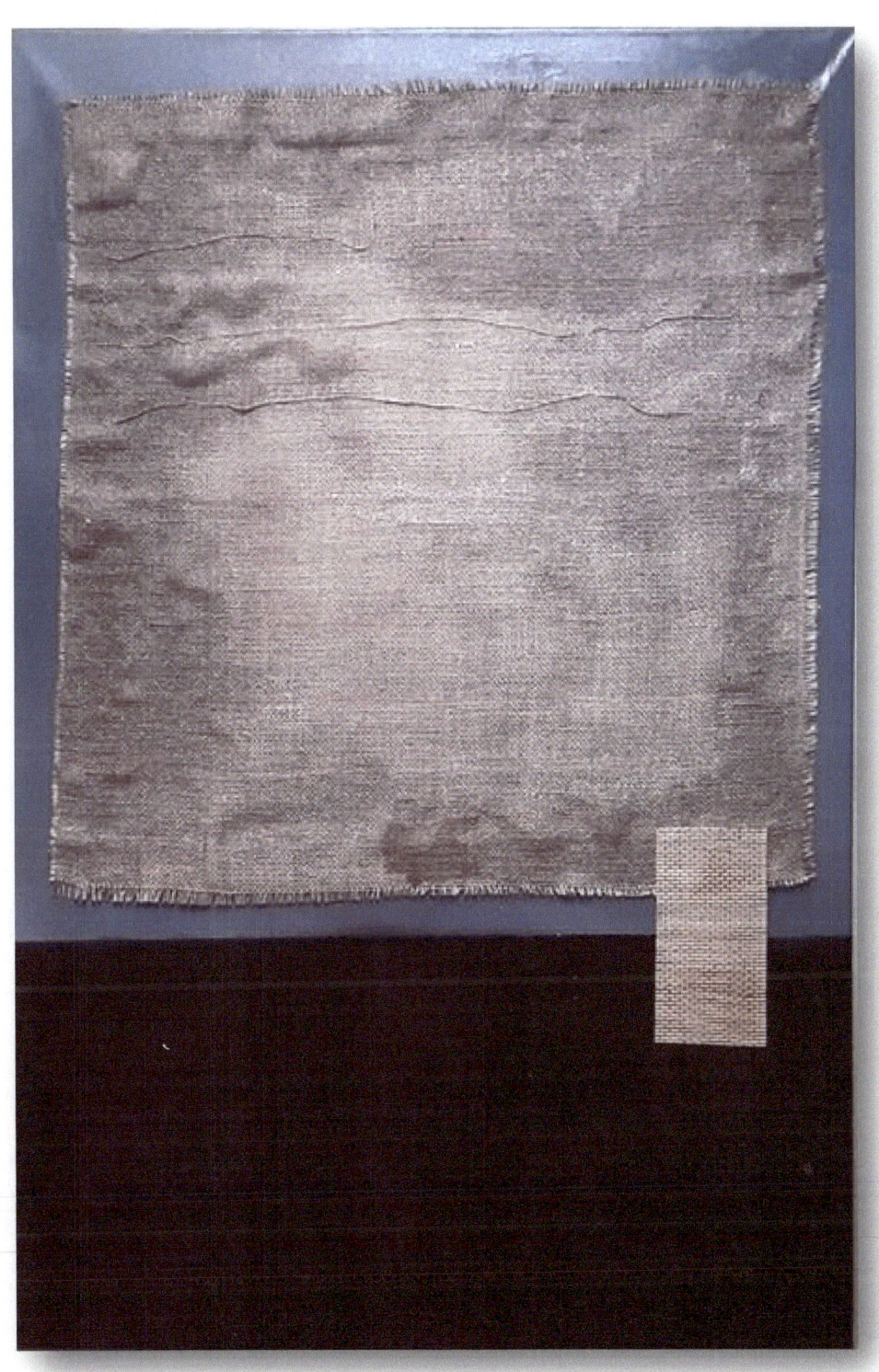

Burlap and acrylic on canvas, 100 by 70 cm

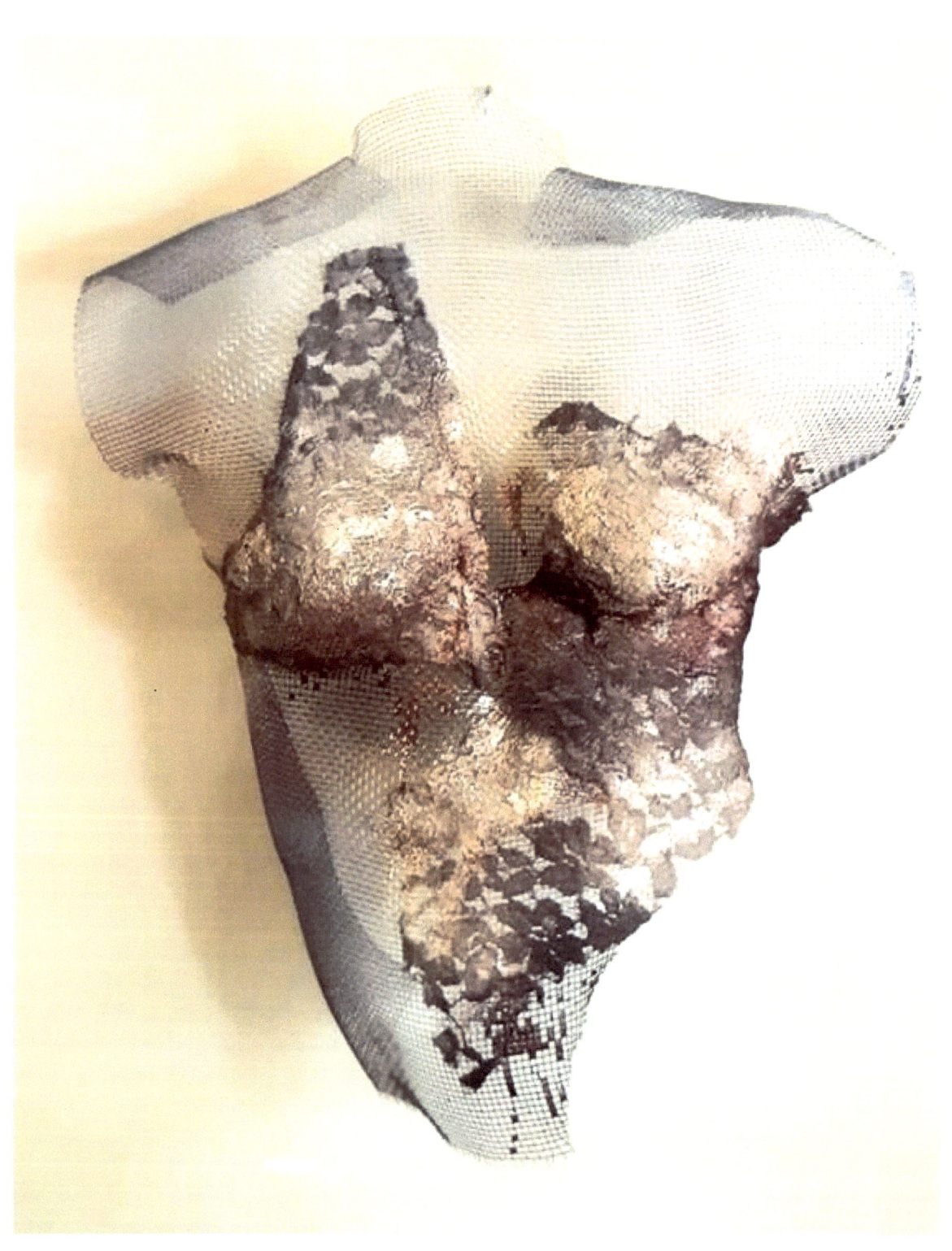

Grid sculpture, 40 by 40 cm

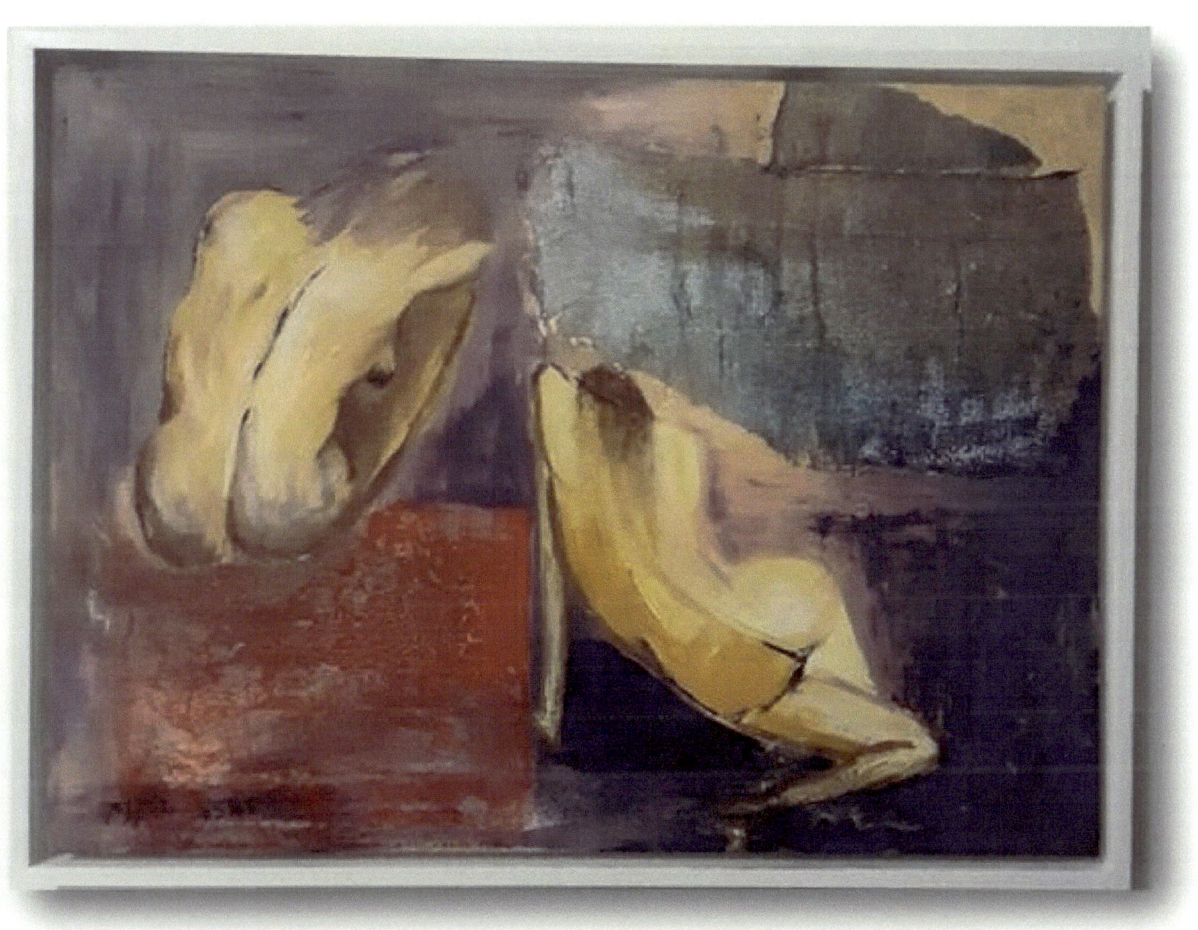

Mix Media Acrylic on canvas, 54 by 74 cm

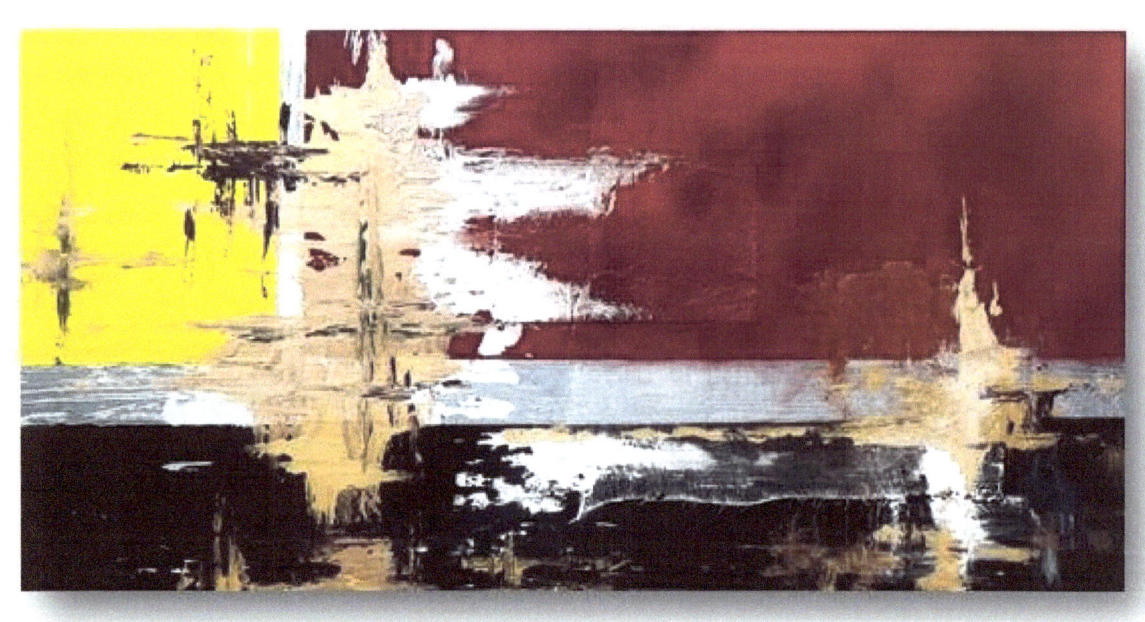

Acrylic and fabric on canvas, 50 by 100 cm

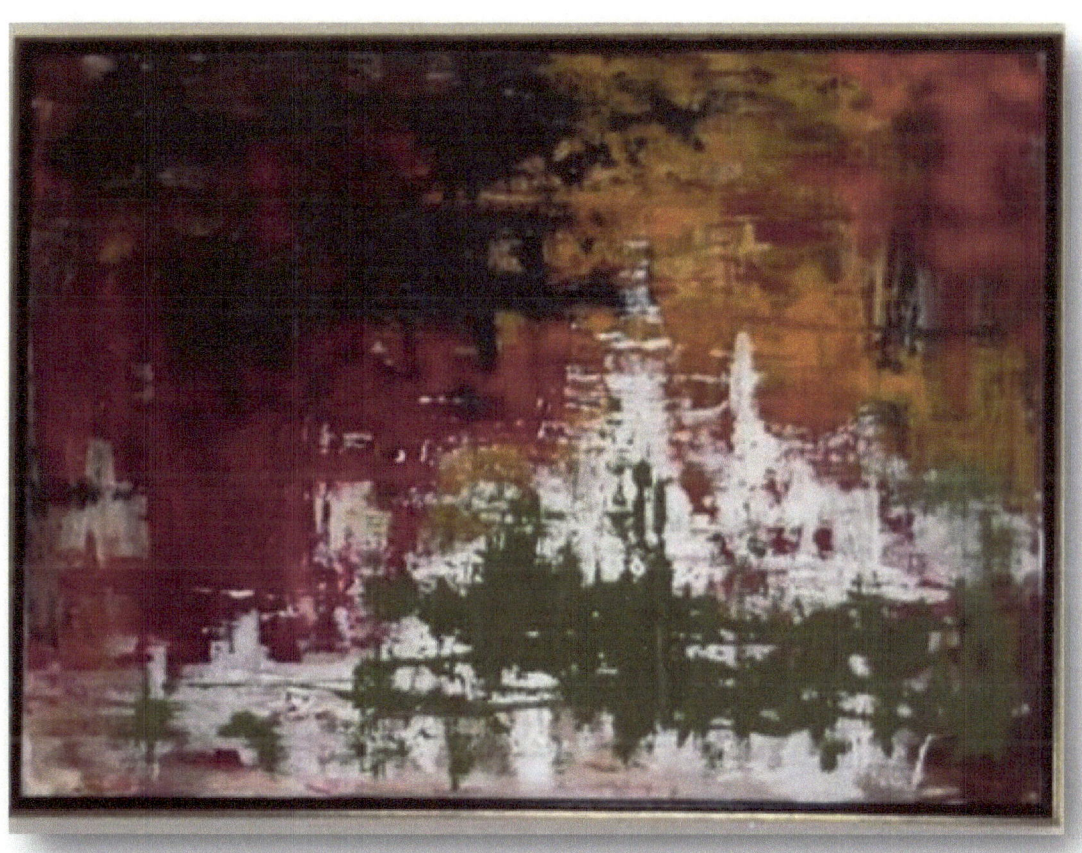

Acrylic on canvas, 52 by 72 cm

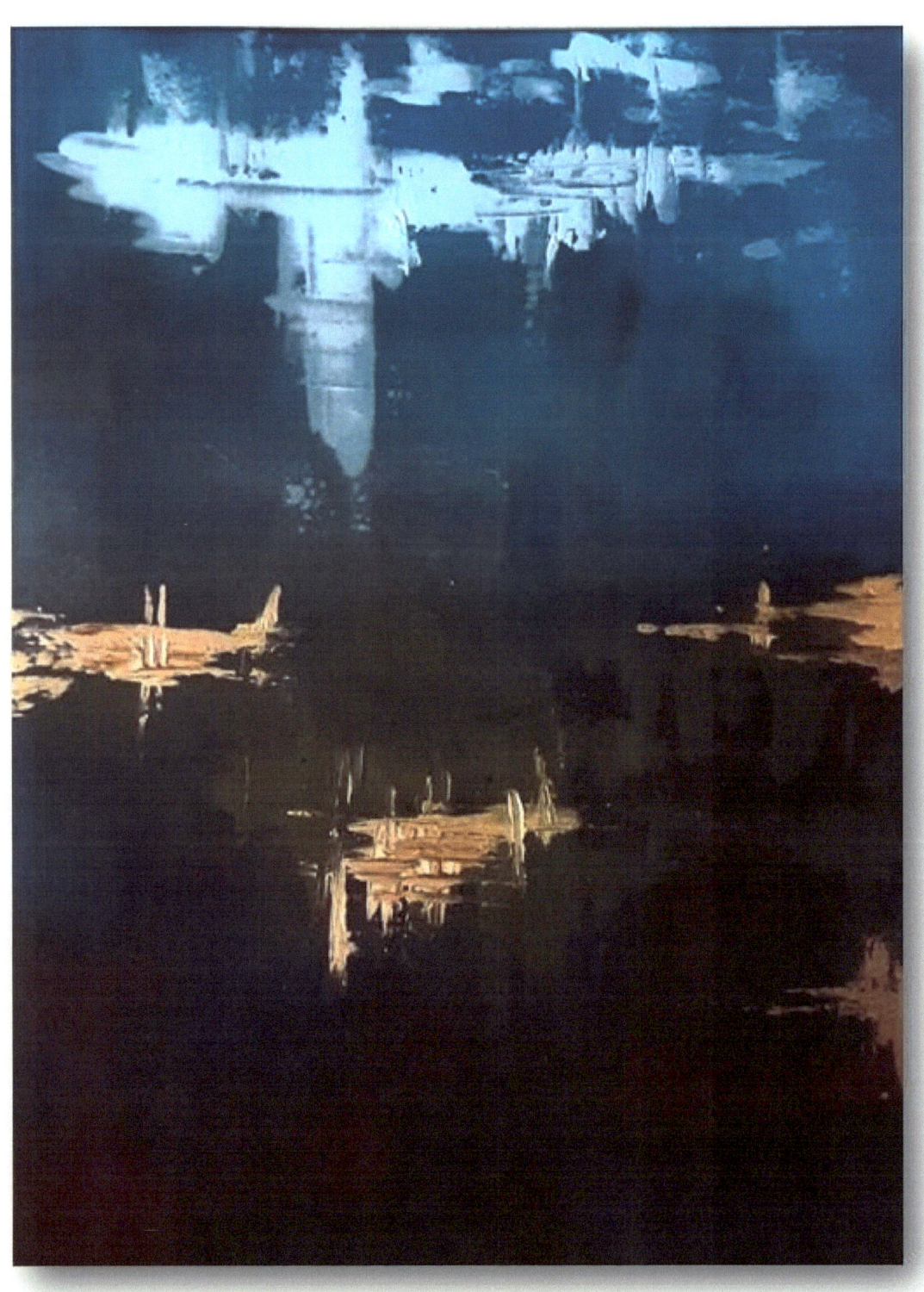

Acrylic on canvas, 90 by 70 cm

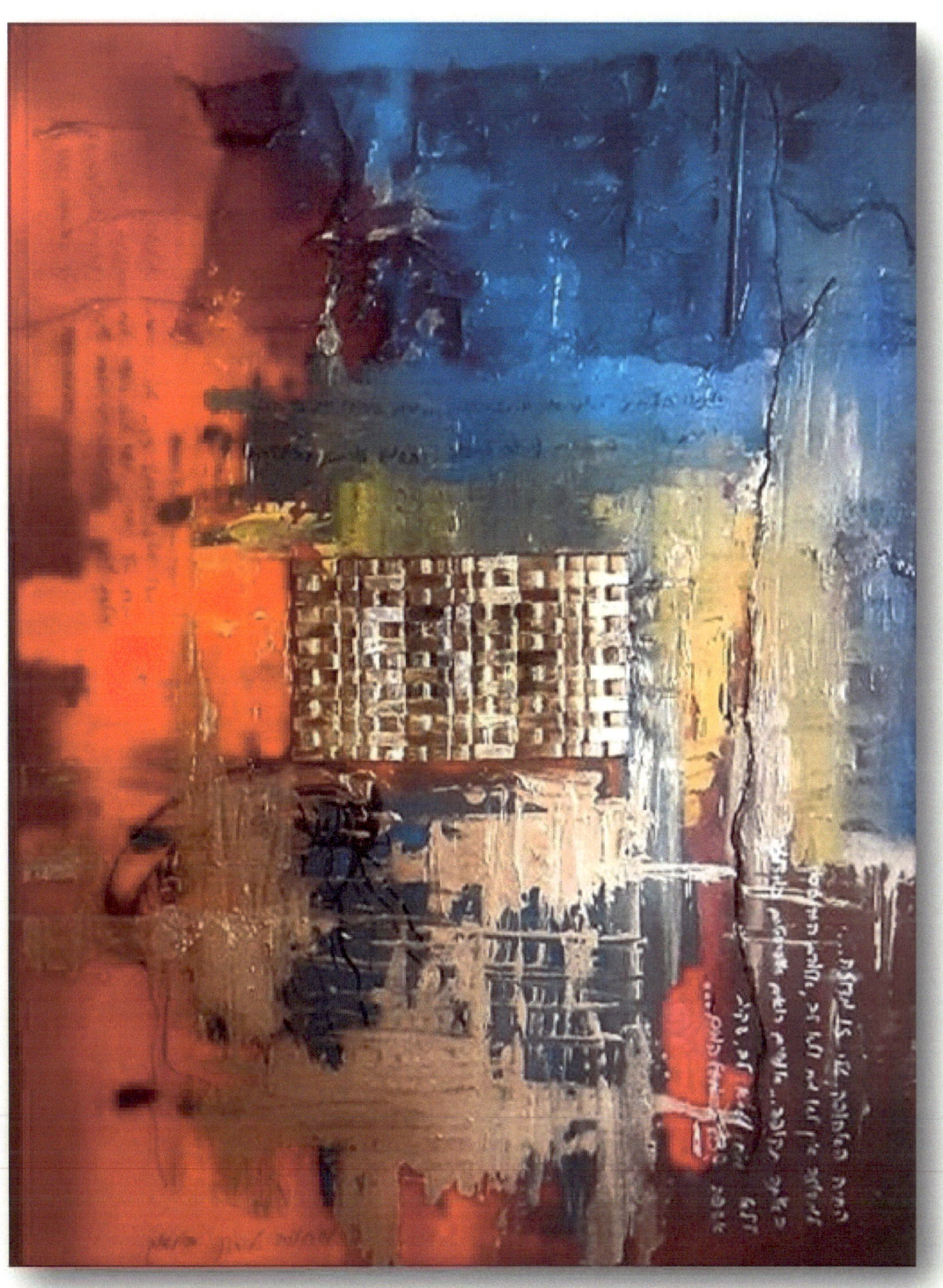

Acrylic on canvas, 90 by 70 cm

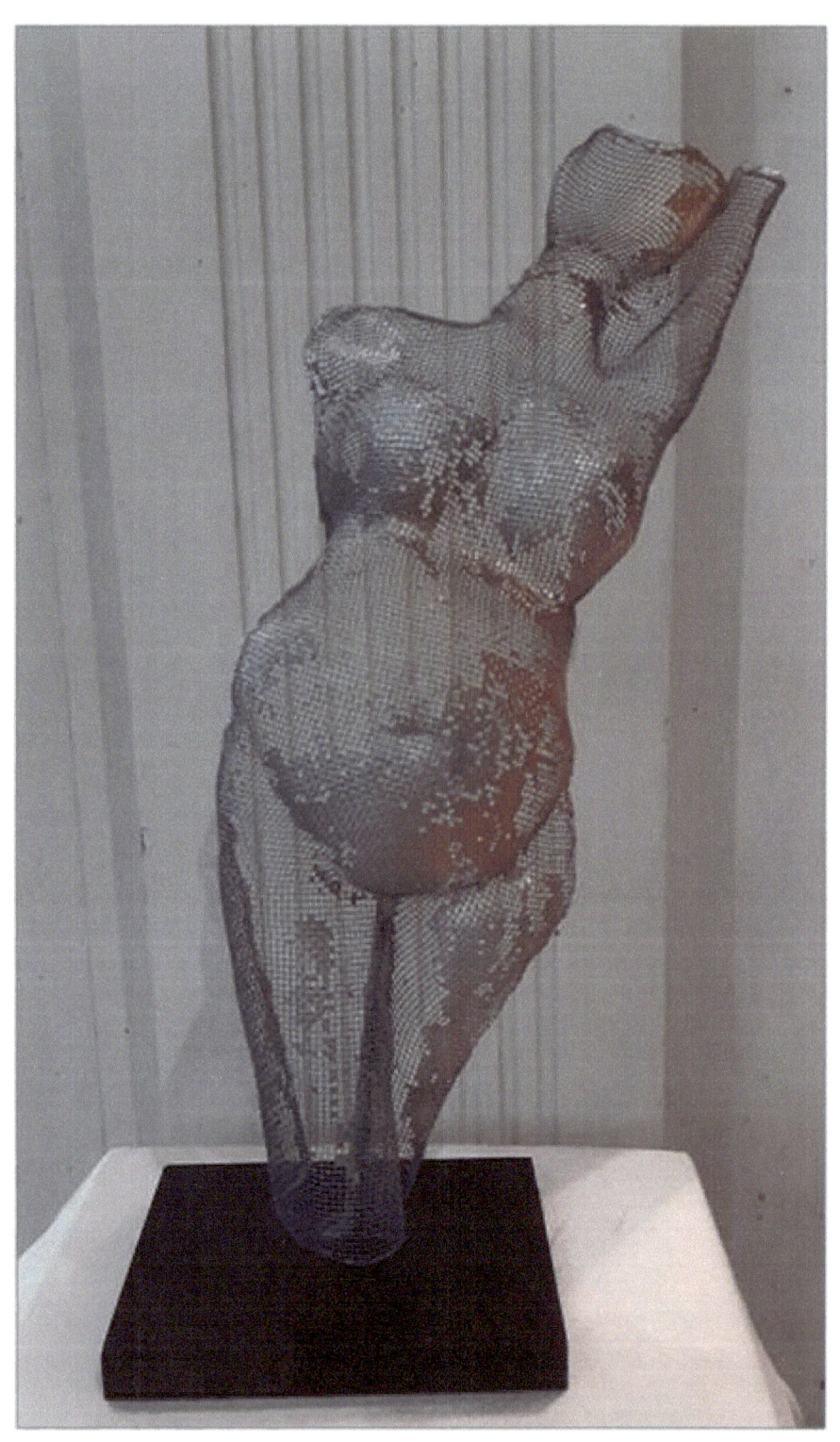

Grid sculpture, 45 cm high

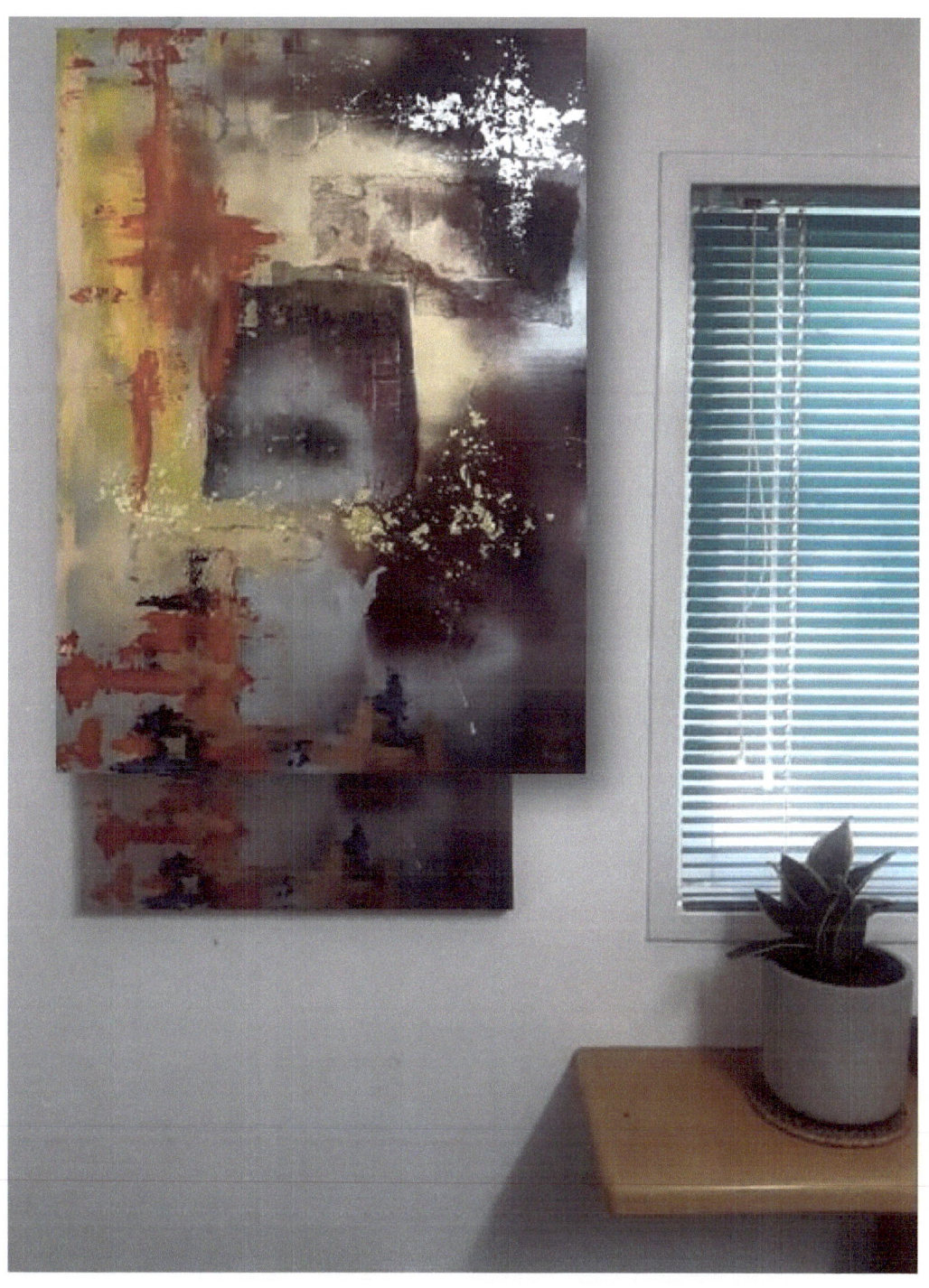

Acrylic on canvas, 90 by 70 cm

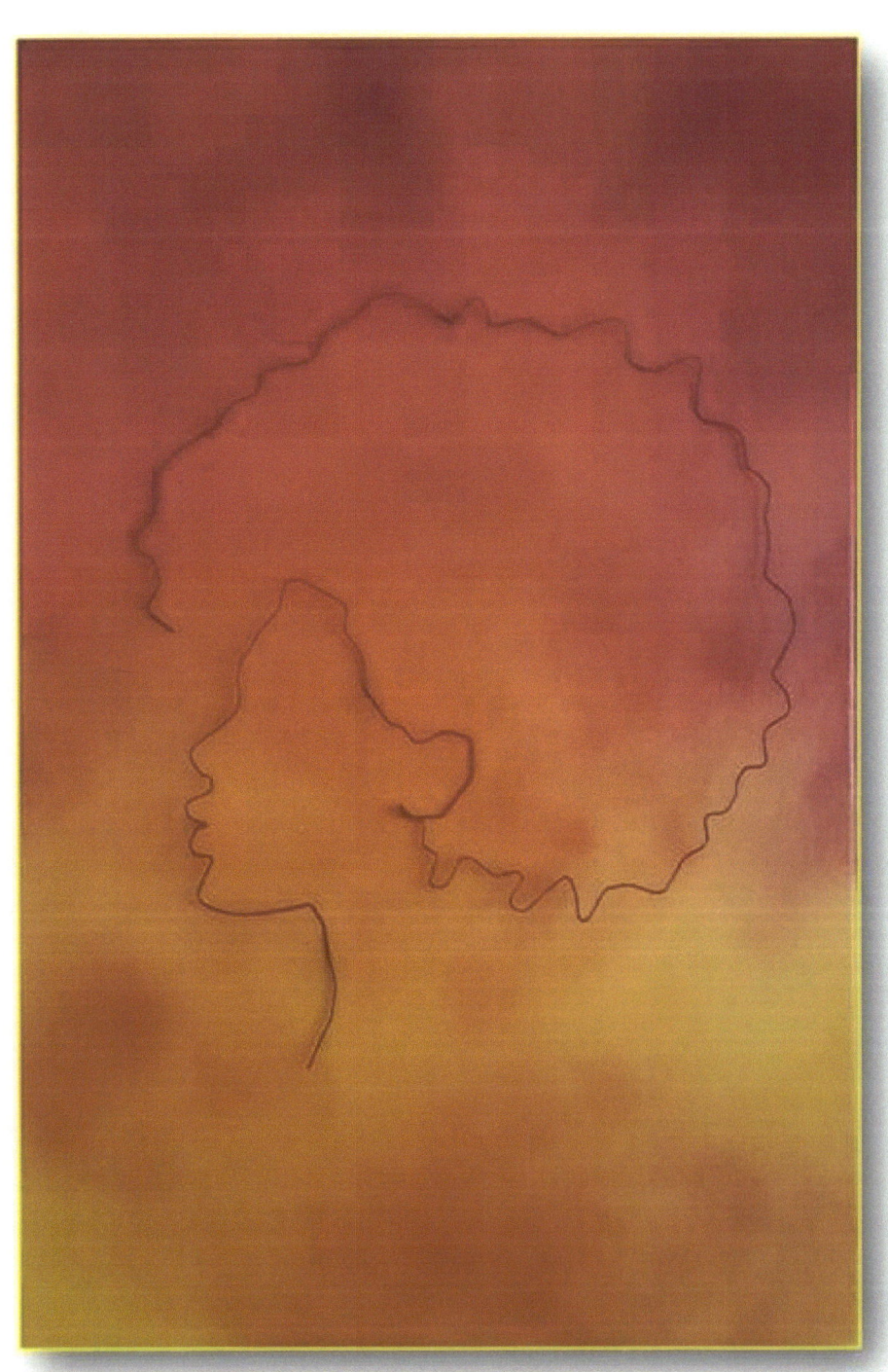

Metal thread end acrylic
on canvas 60 by 40 cm

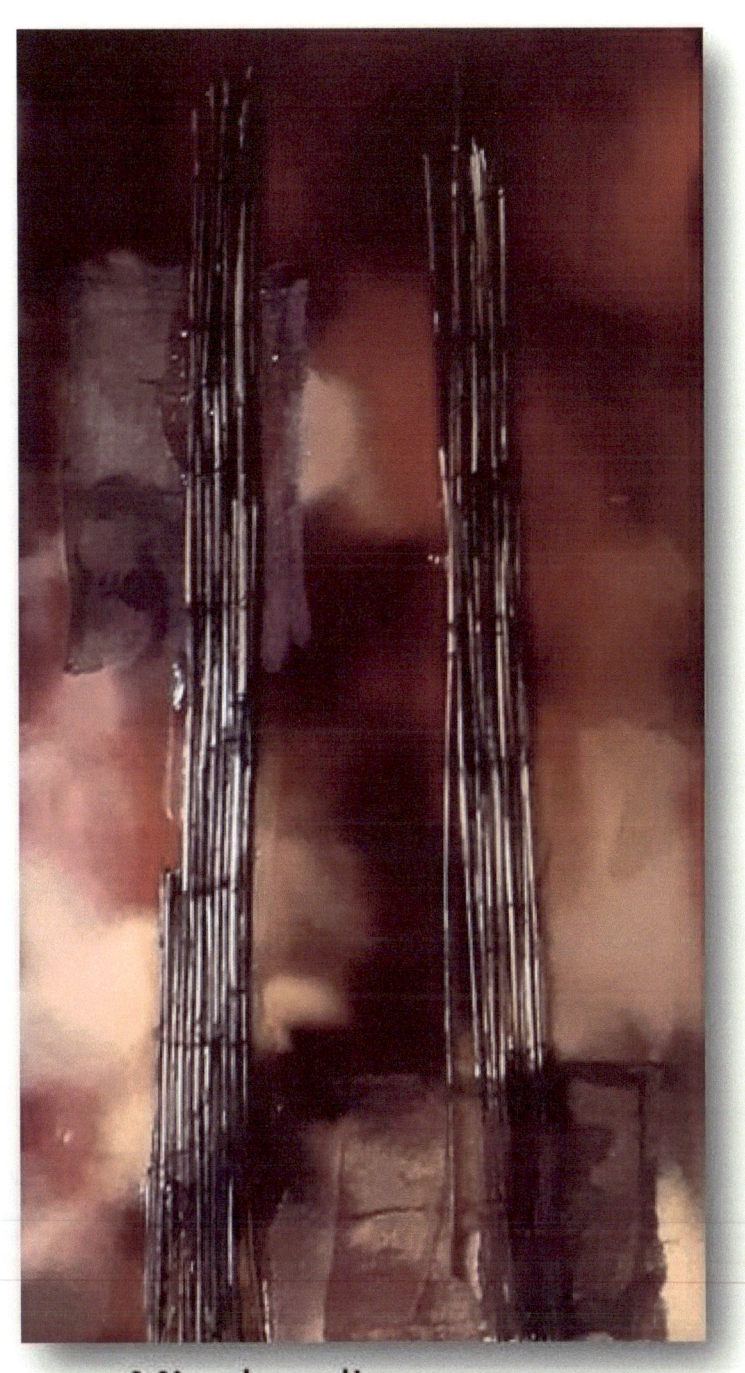

Mixed media on canvas,
50 by 100 cm

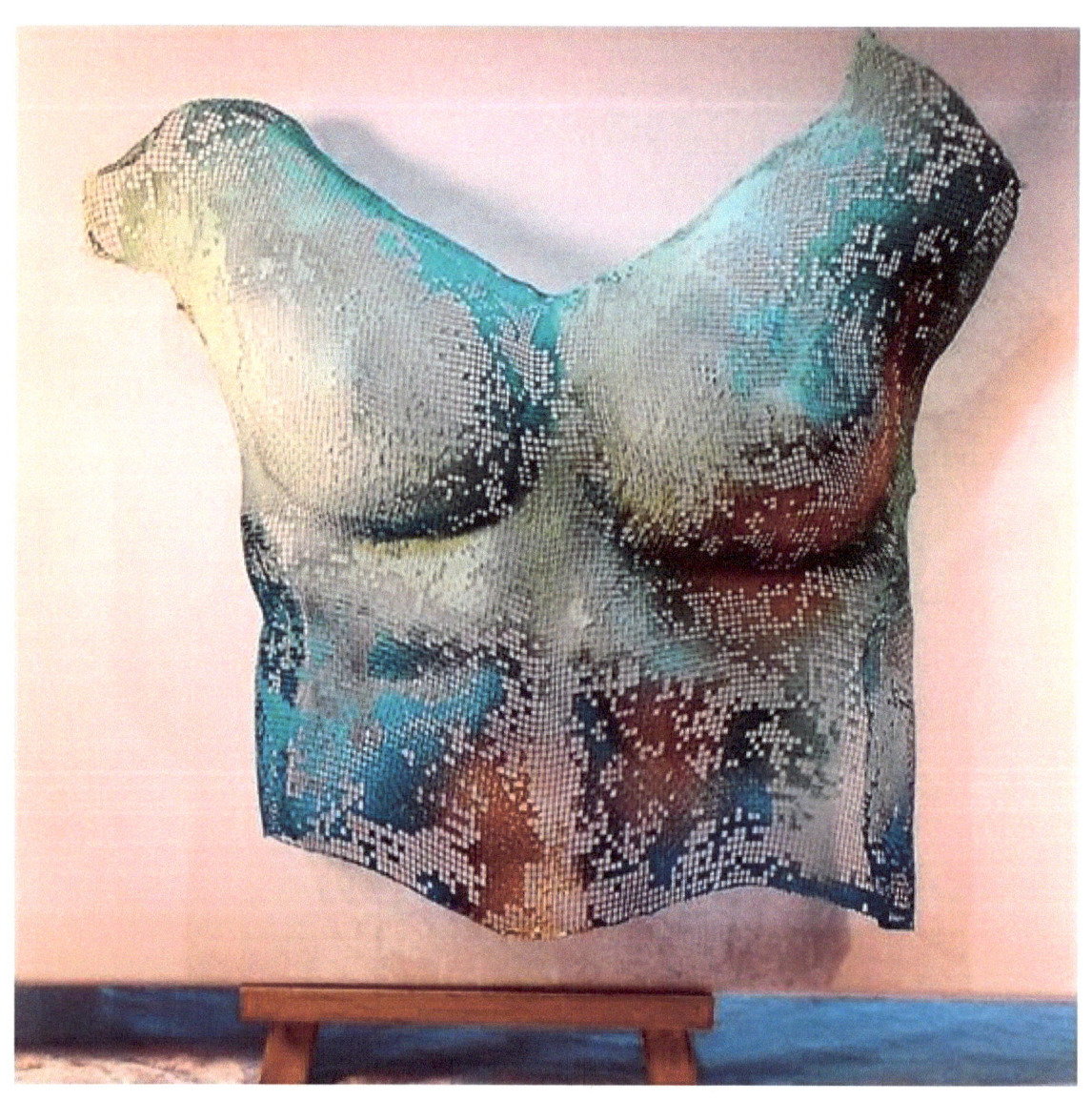

Grid sculpture

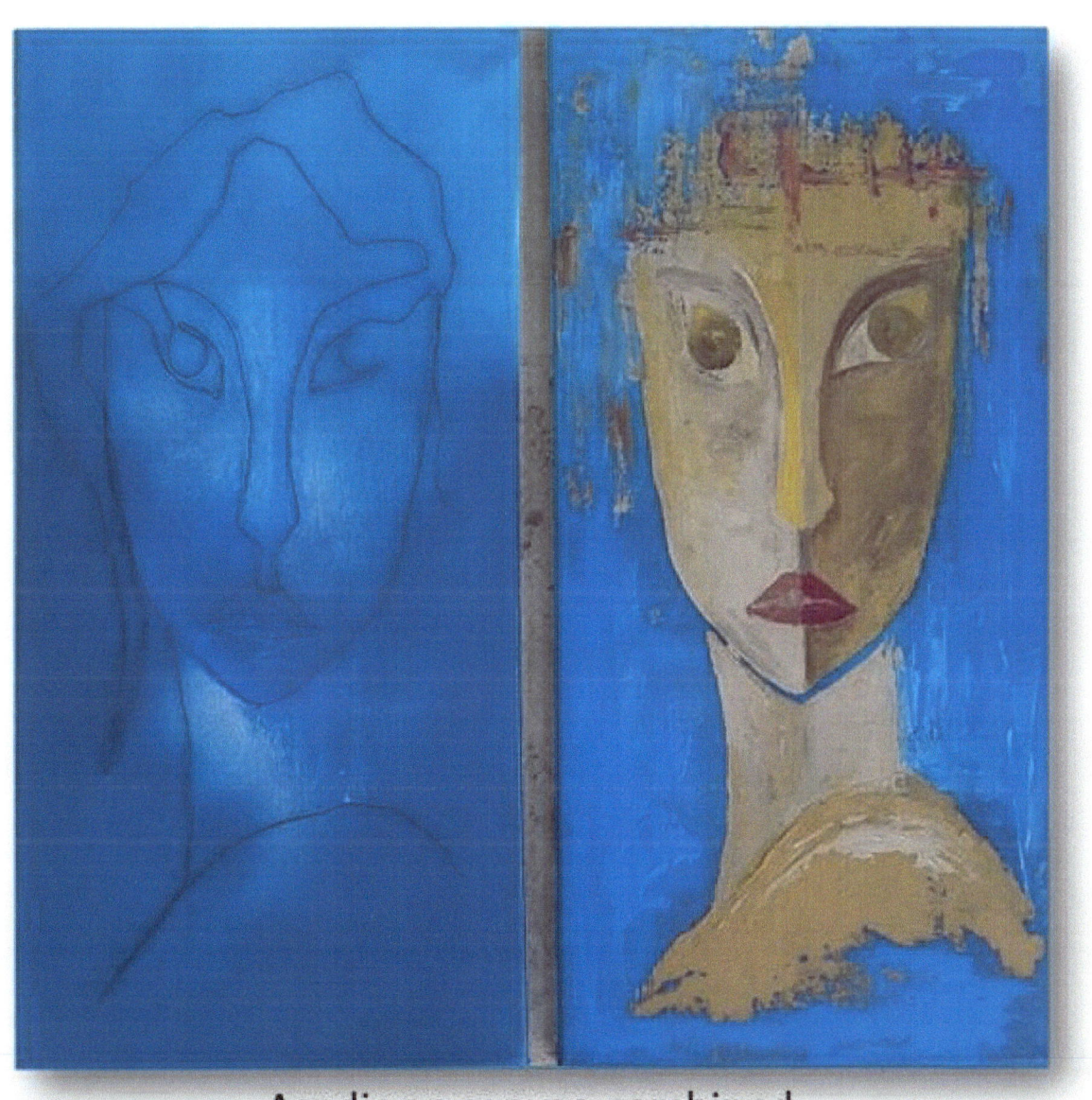

Acrylic on canvas, combined with metal wire, 60 by 30 X2

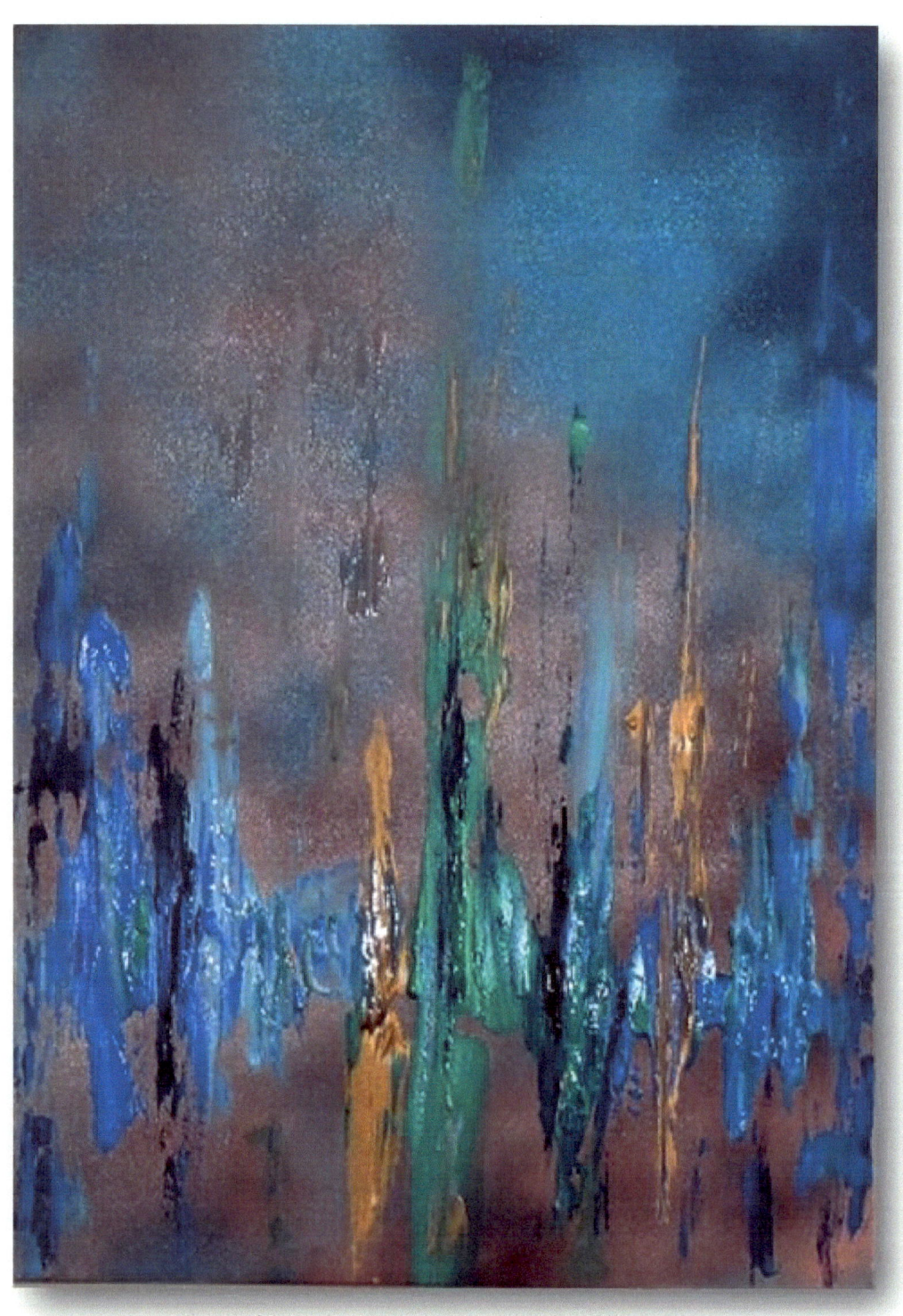

Acrylic on canvas, 70 by 50 cm

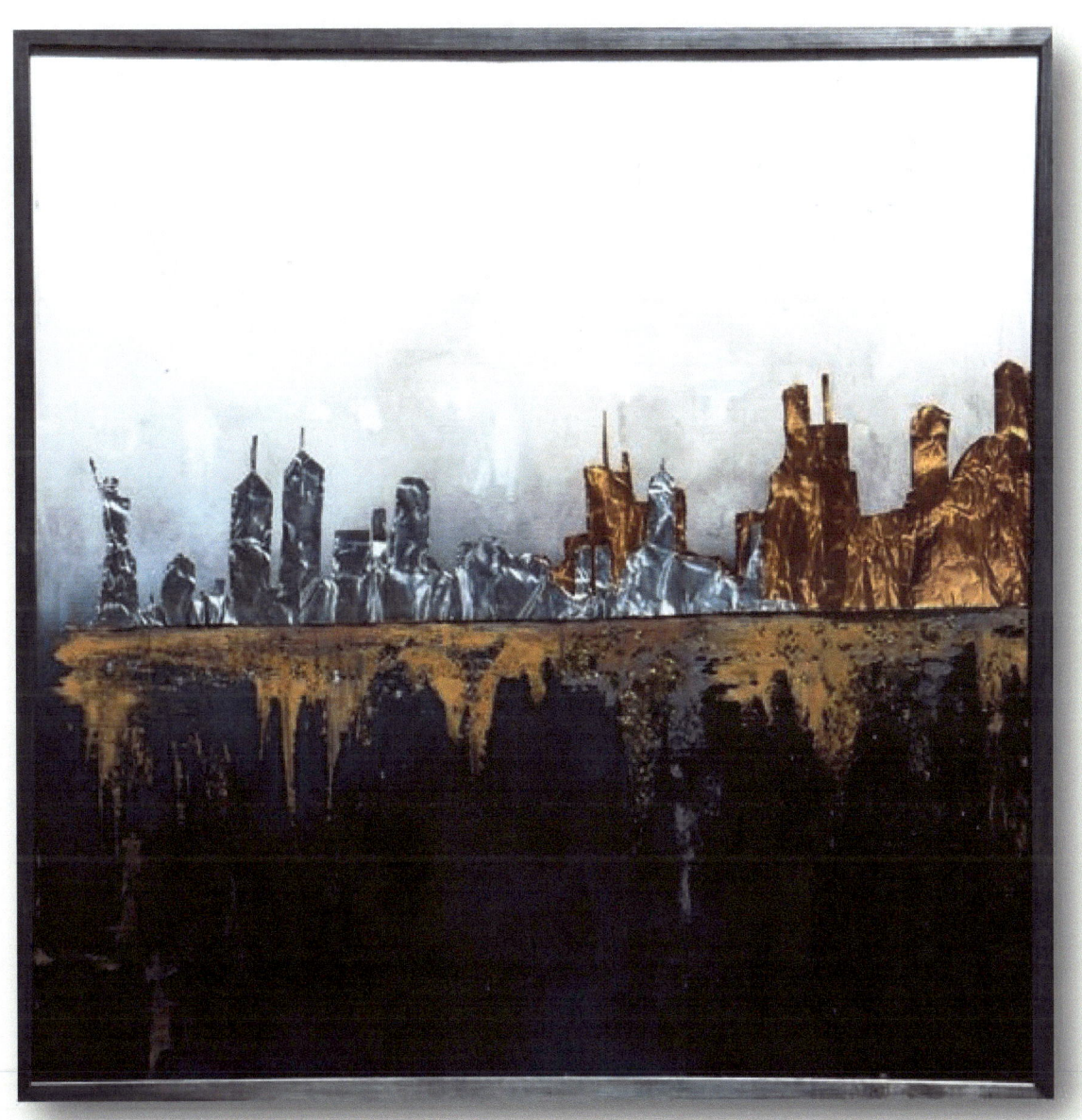

Mixed media on canvas, 80 by 80 cm

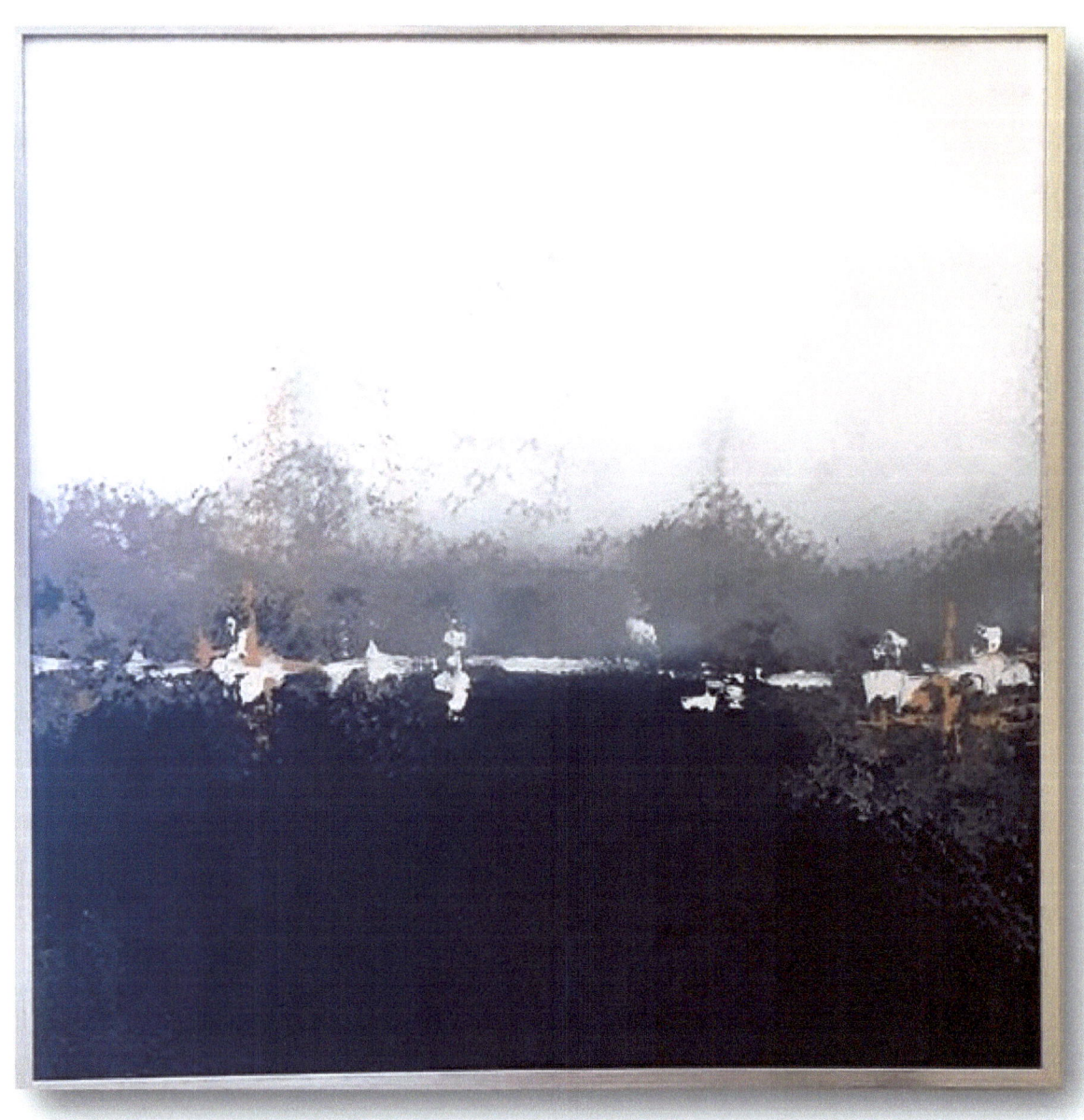

Acrylic on canvas, 80 by 80 cm

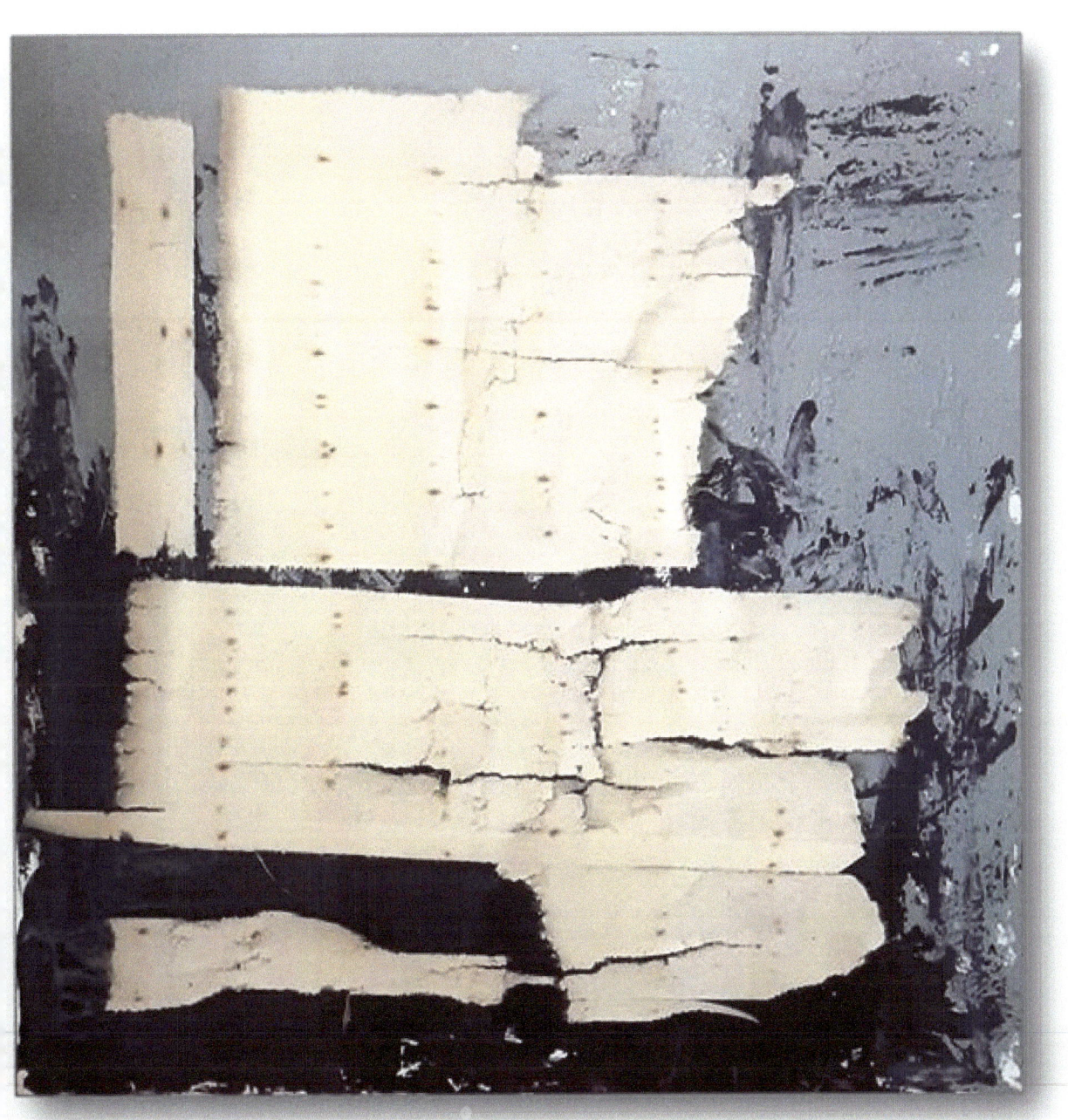

Mixed media on canvas, 90 by 90 cm

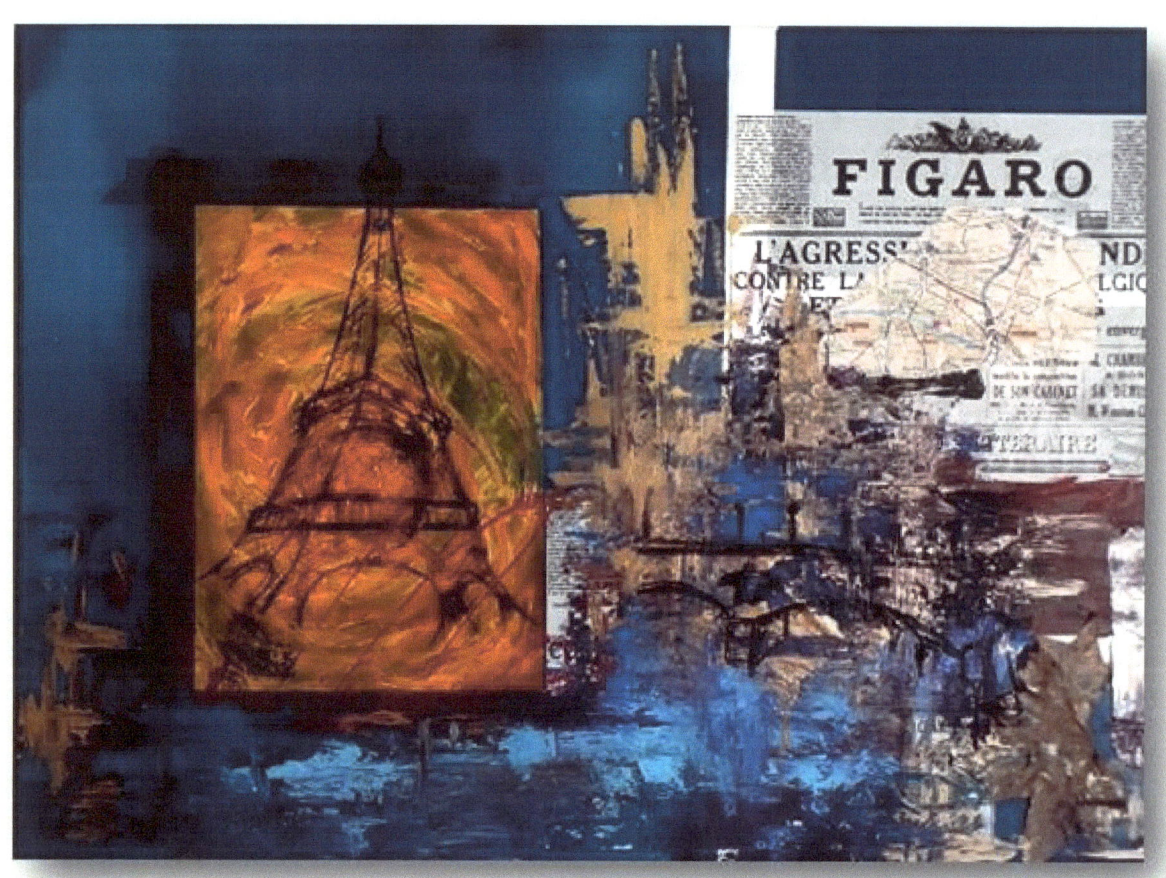

Mixed media on canvas, 70 by 100 cm

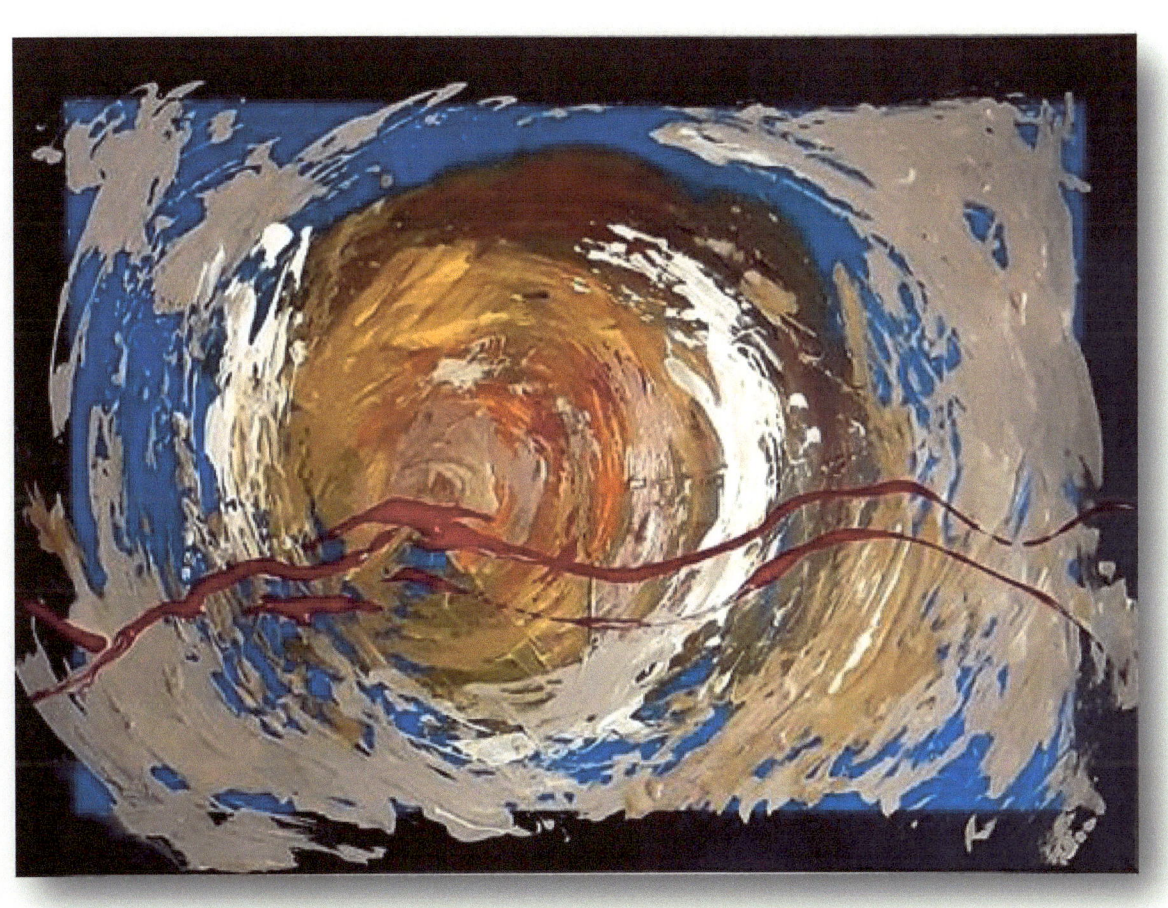

Acrylic on canvas, 50 by 70 cm

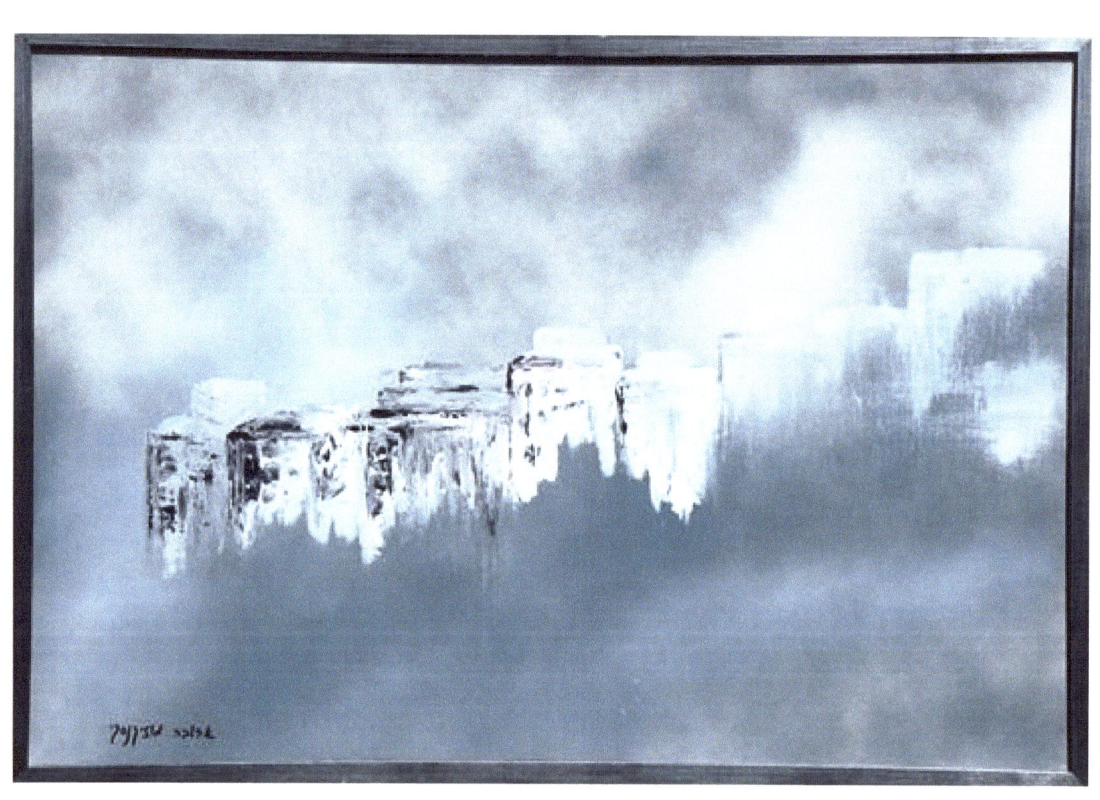

Acrylic on canvas, 63 by 93 cm

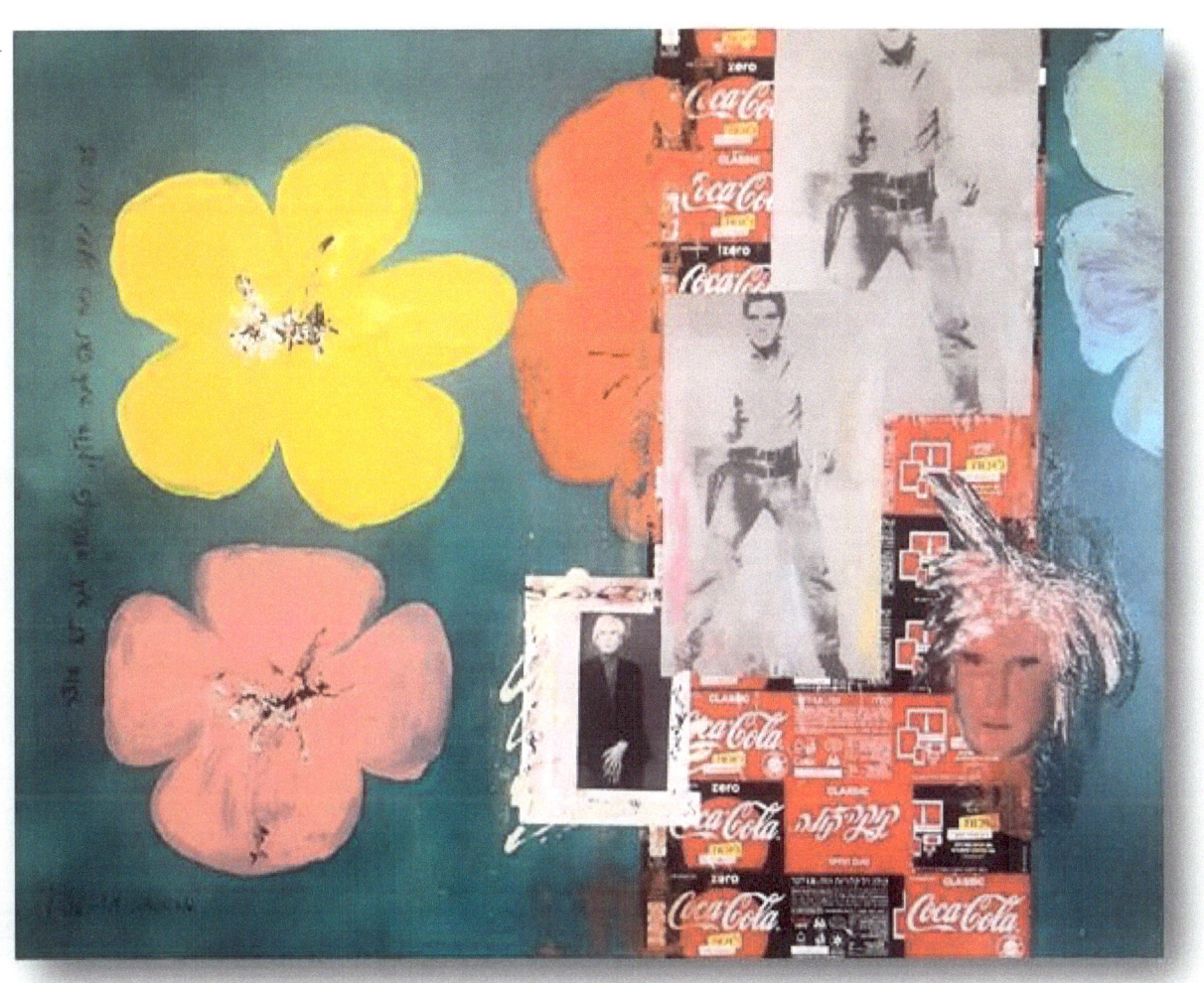

Mixed media on canvas, 68 by 98 cm

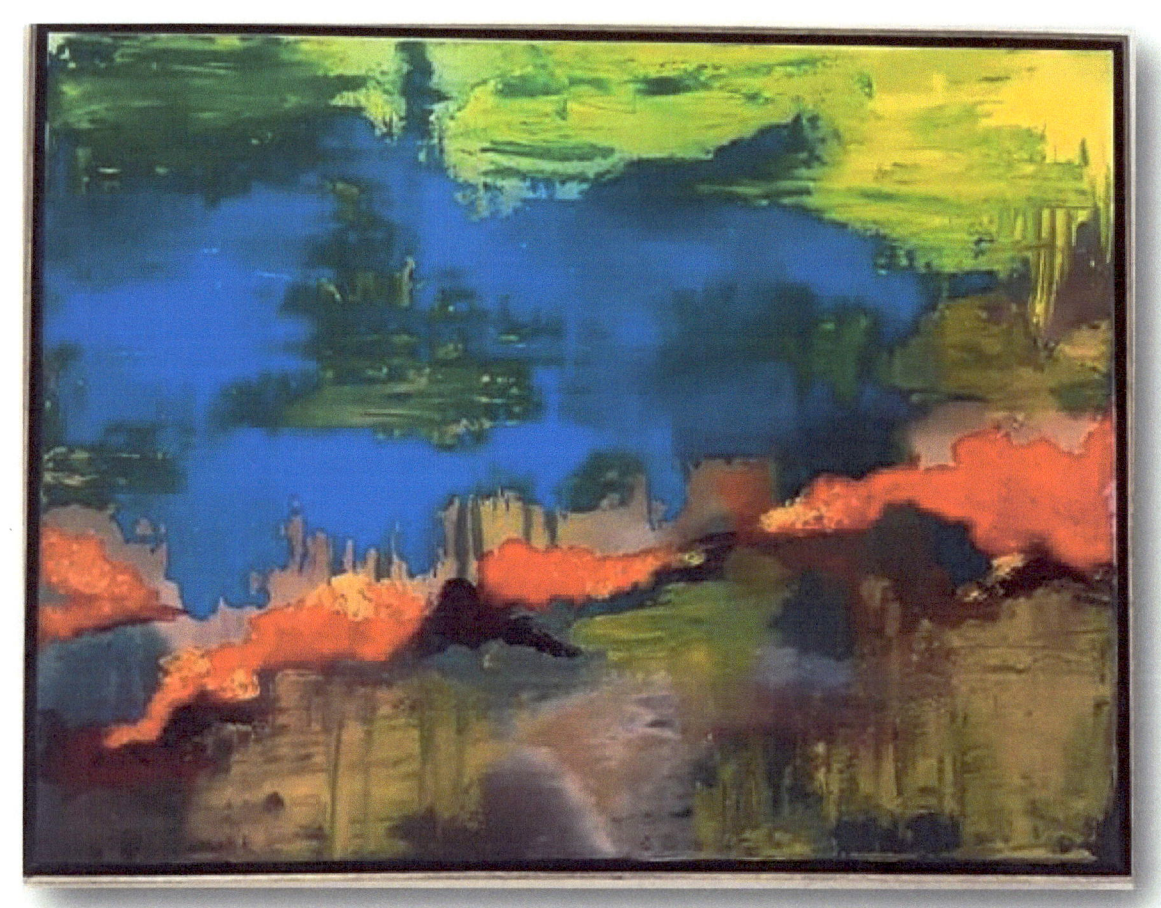

Acrylic on canvas, 50 by 70 cm

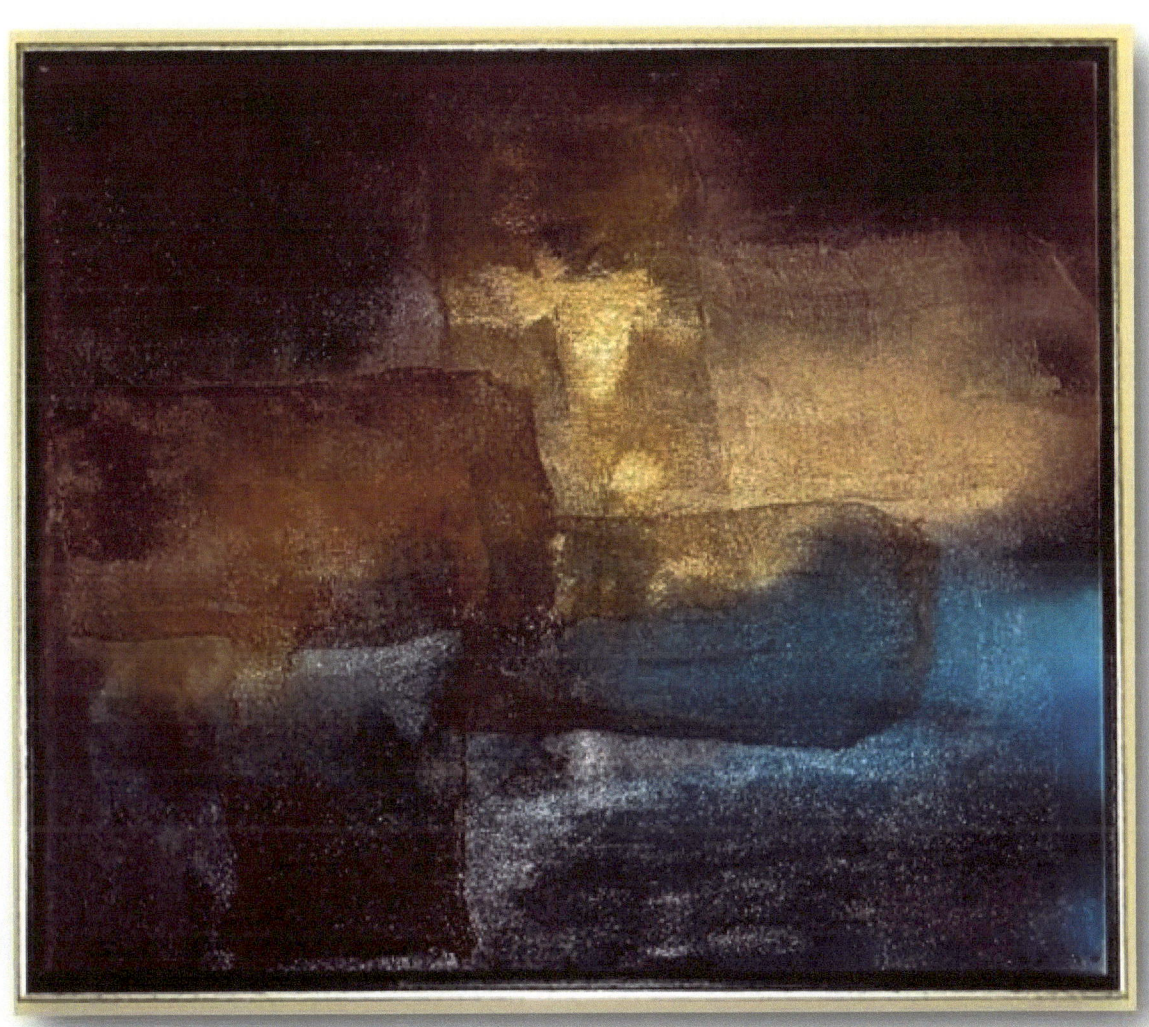

Mixed media on canvas, 50 by 60 cm

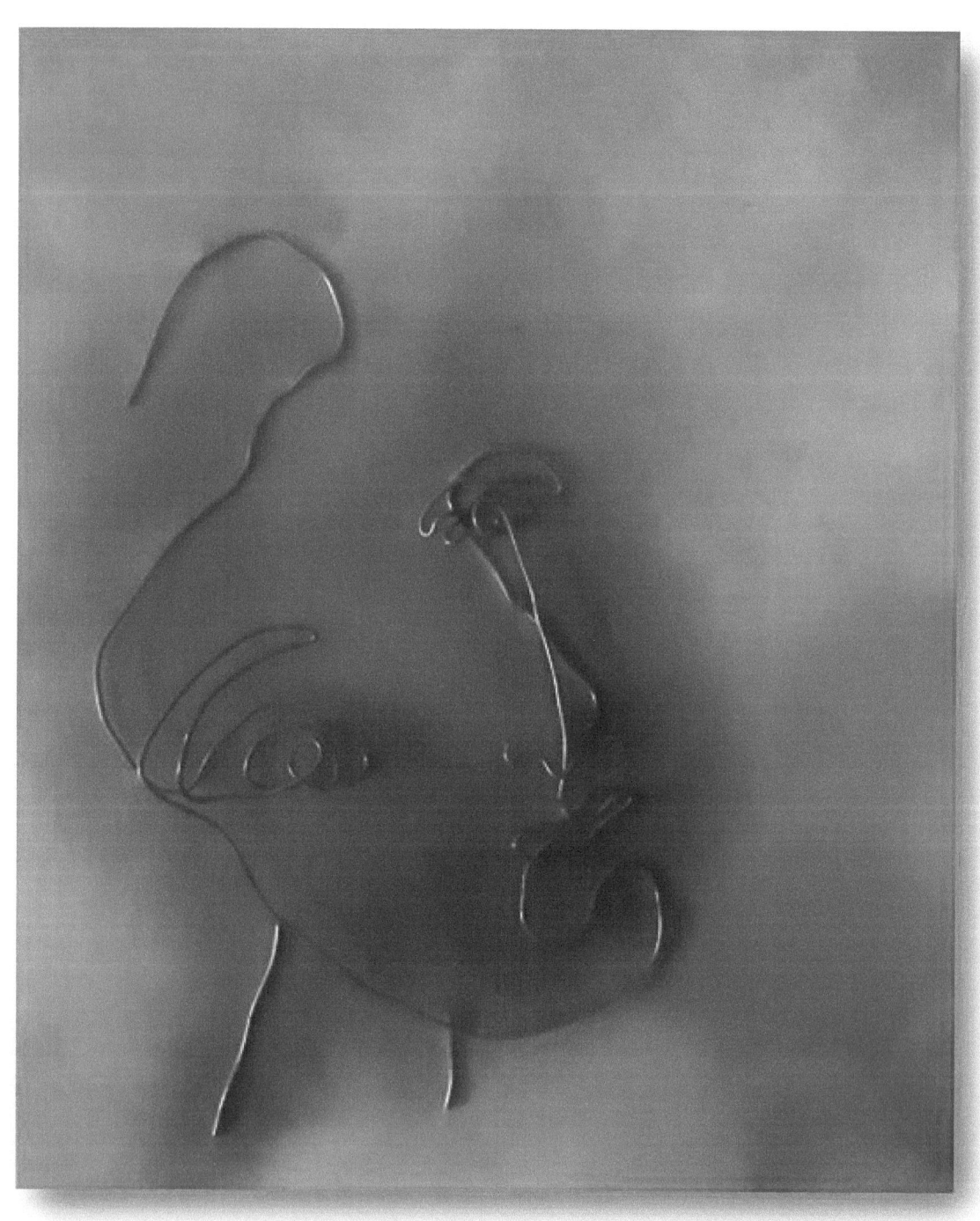

Acrylic and metal thread on canvas, 45 by 40 cm

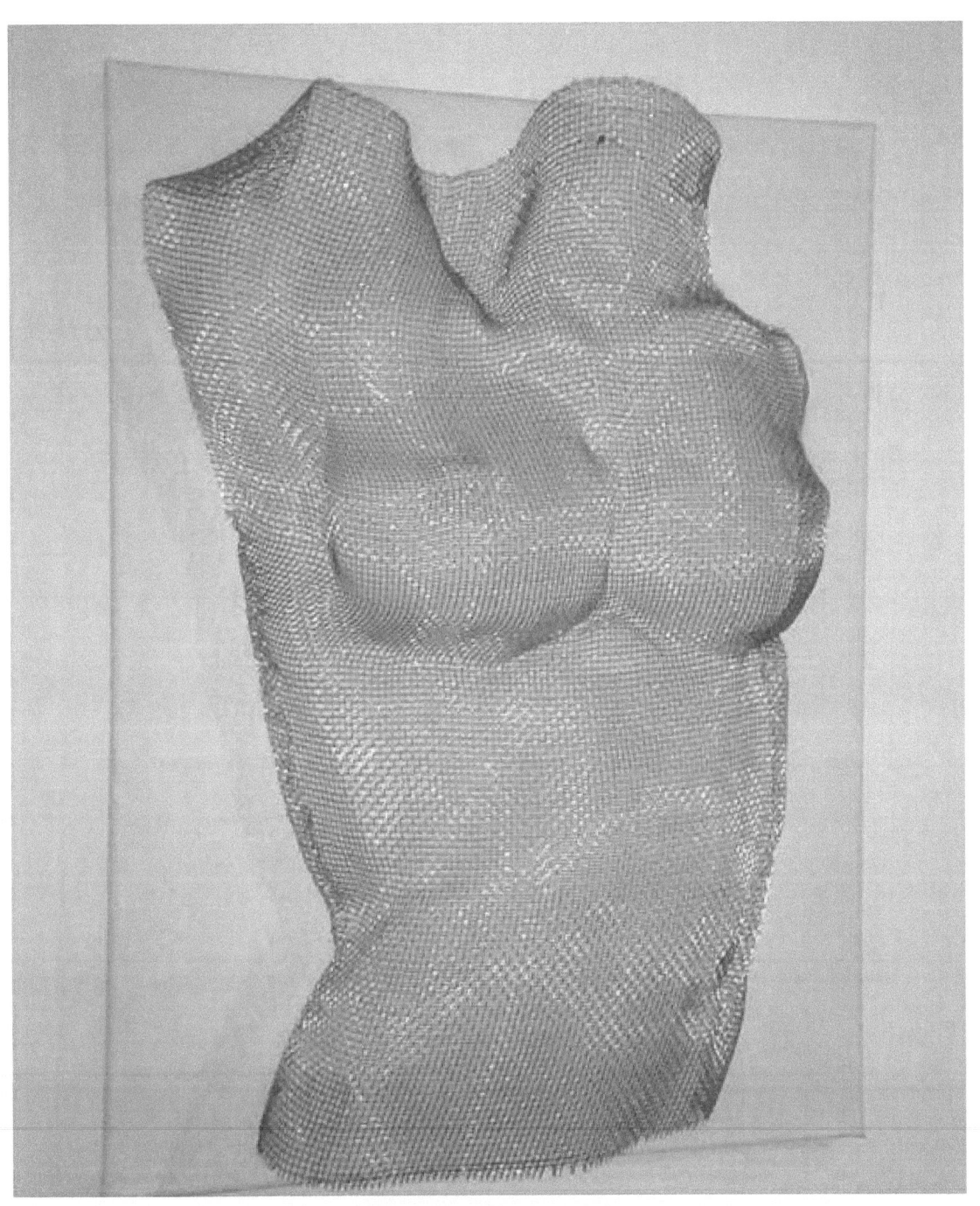

Grid sculpture

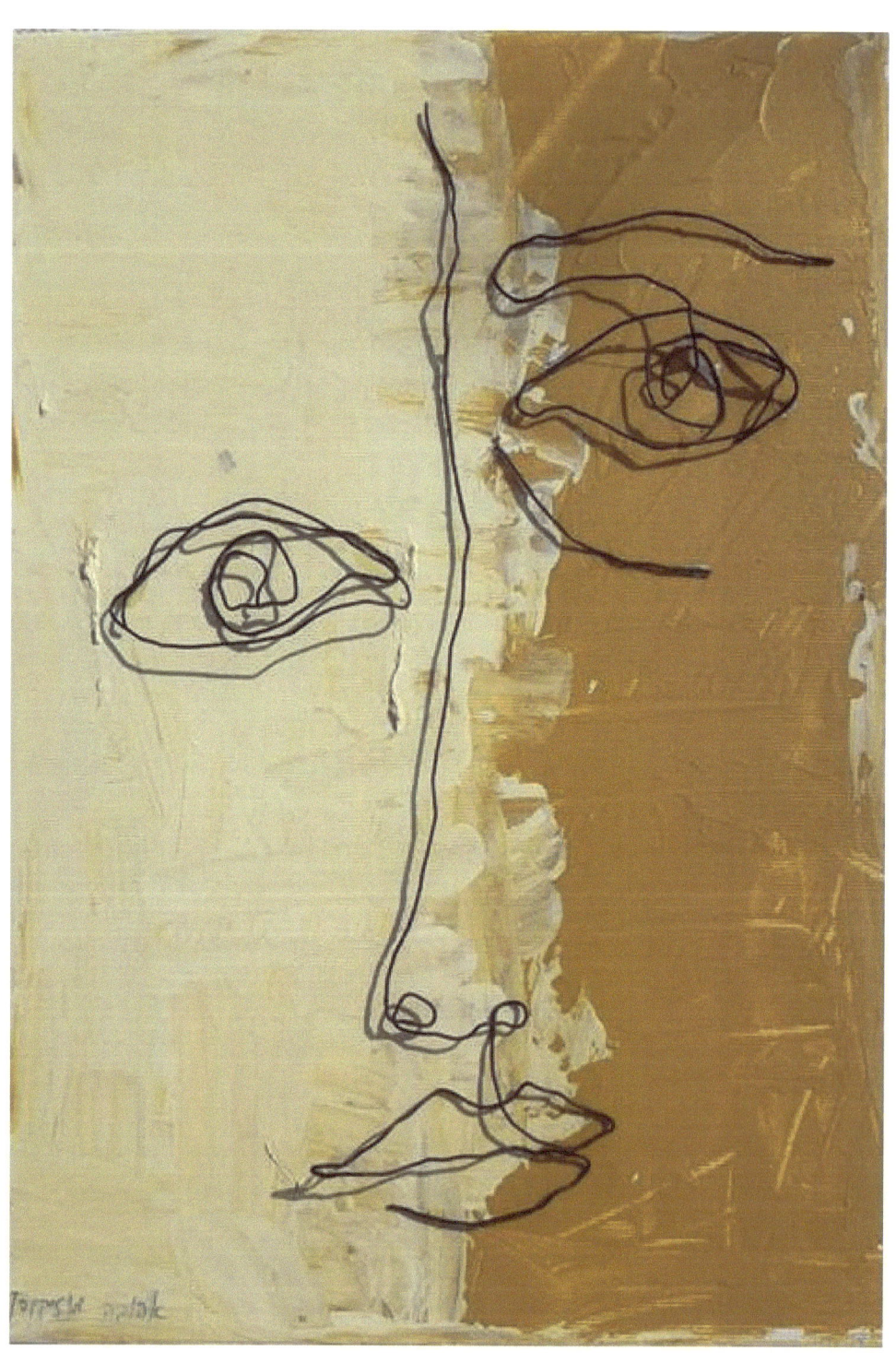

Metal wire and acrylic on canvas, 40 by 30 cm

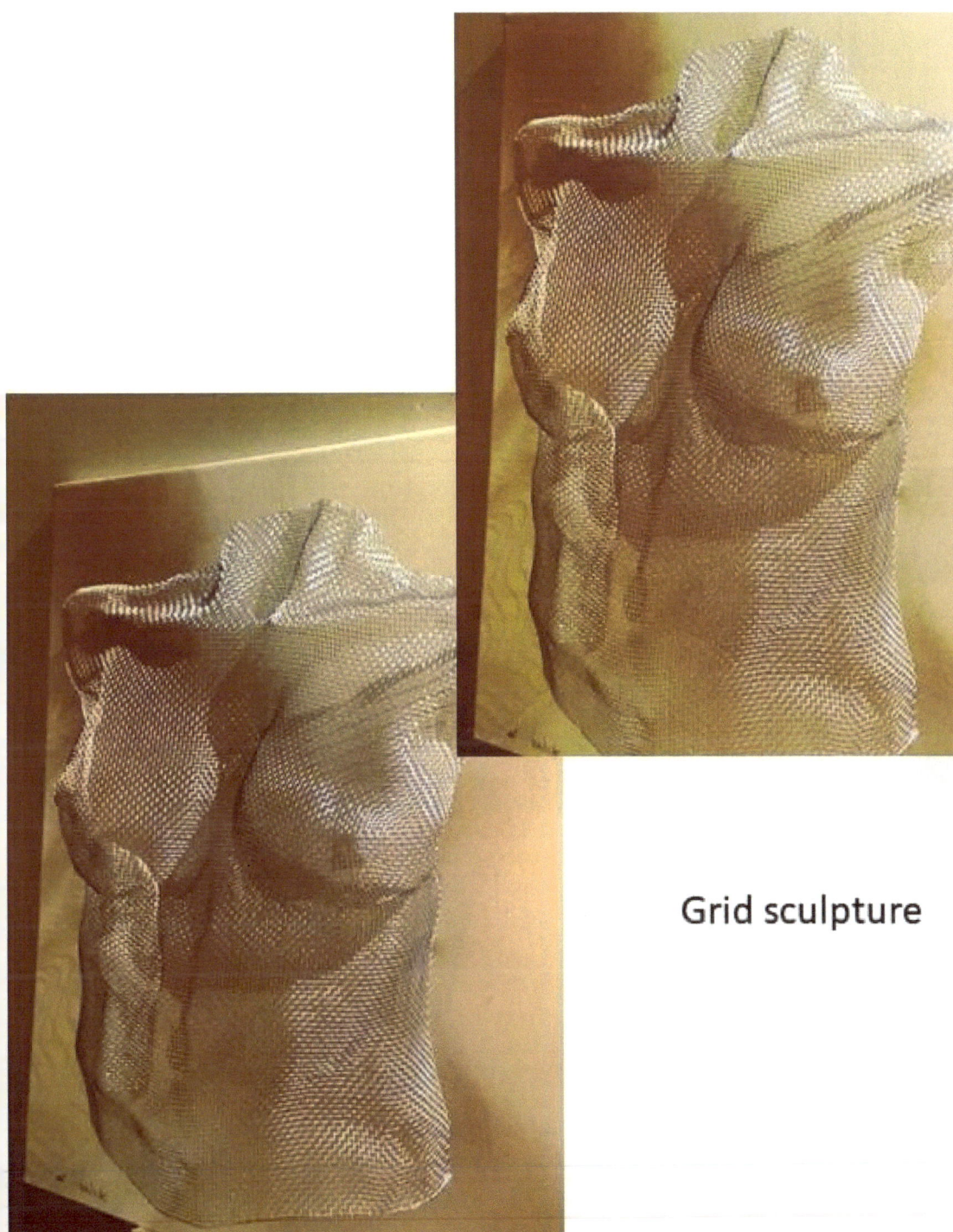

Grid sculpture

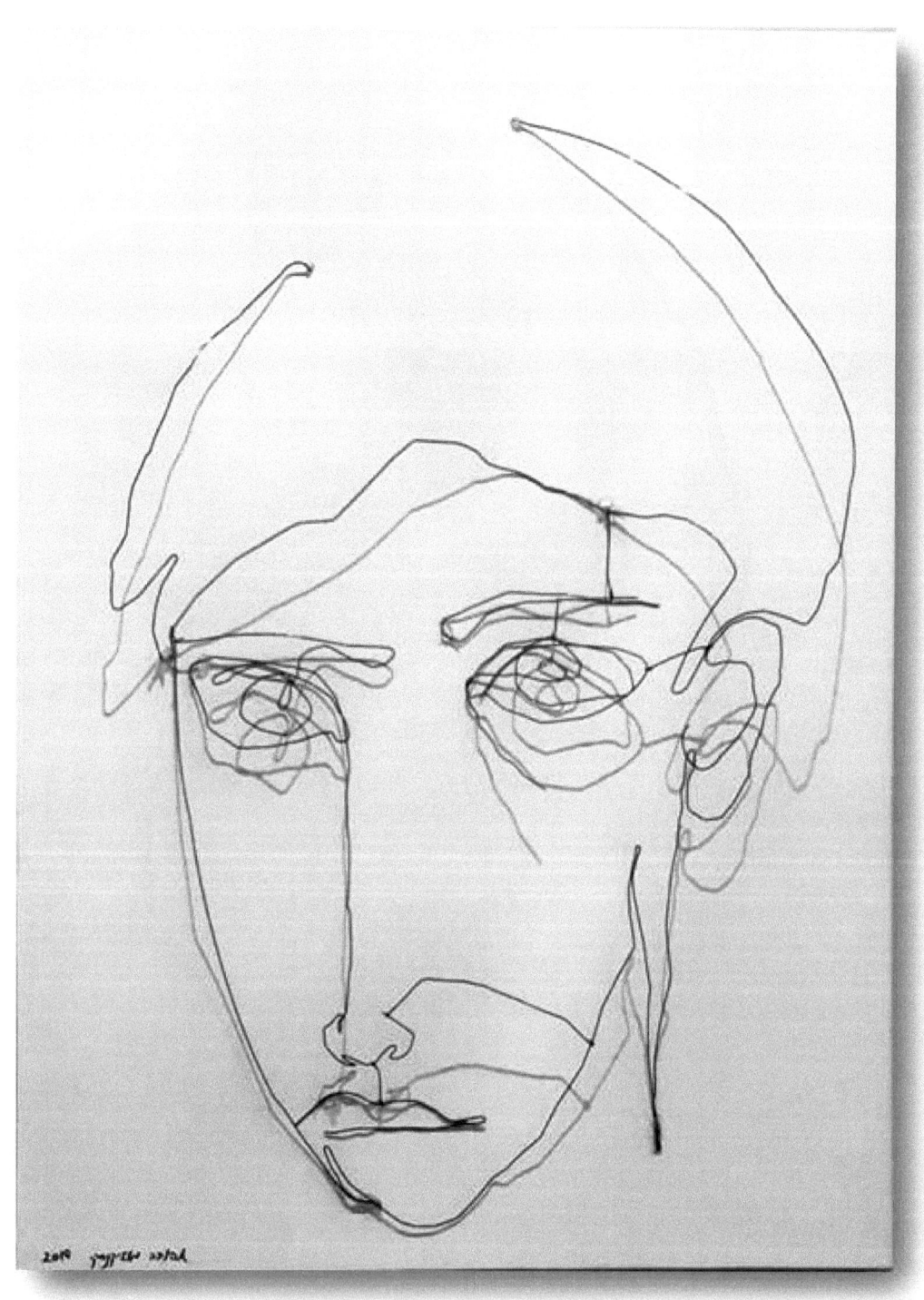

Metal wire sculpture

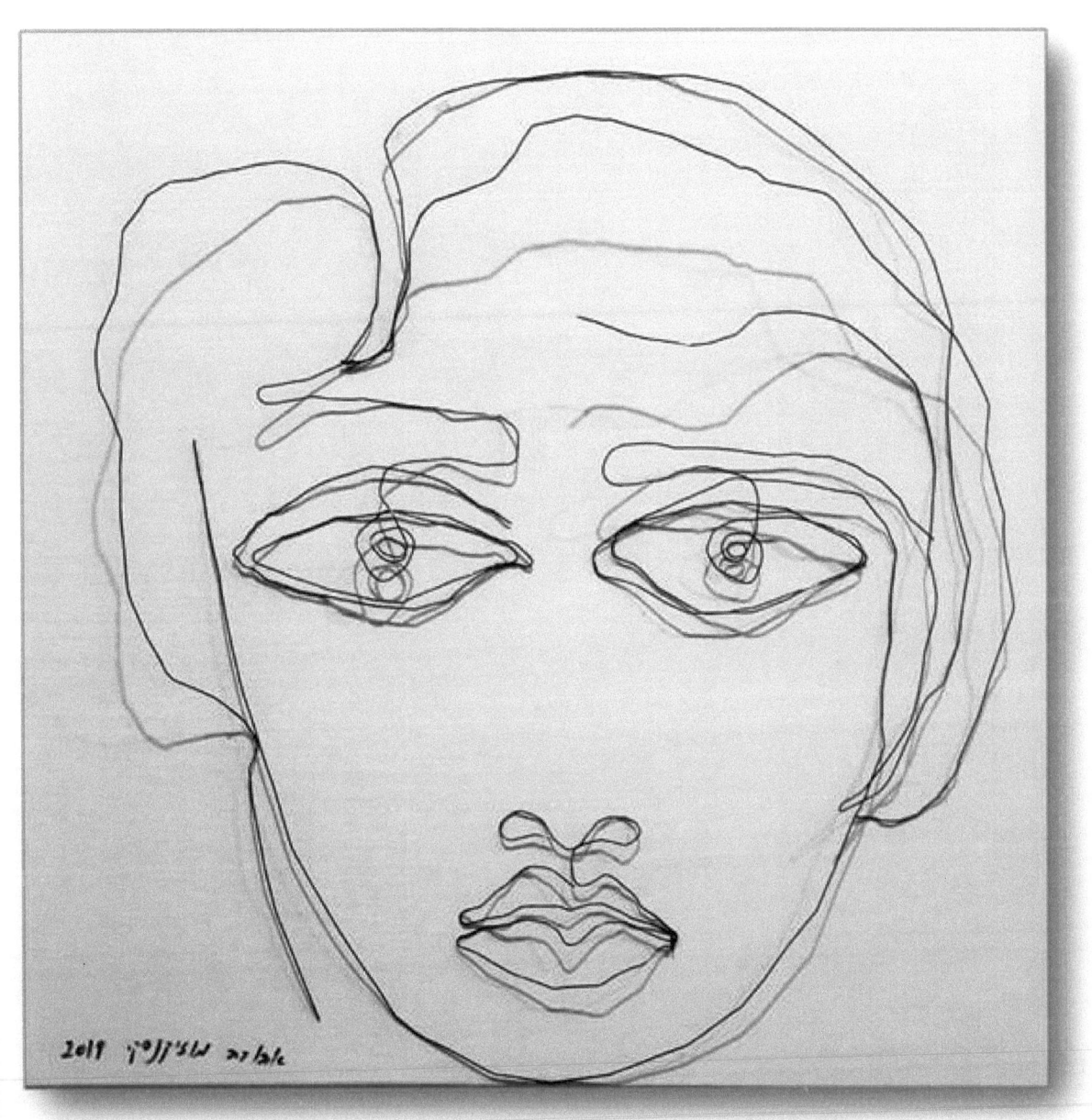

Metal wire sculpture, 50 by 50 cm

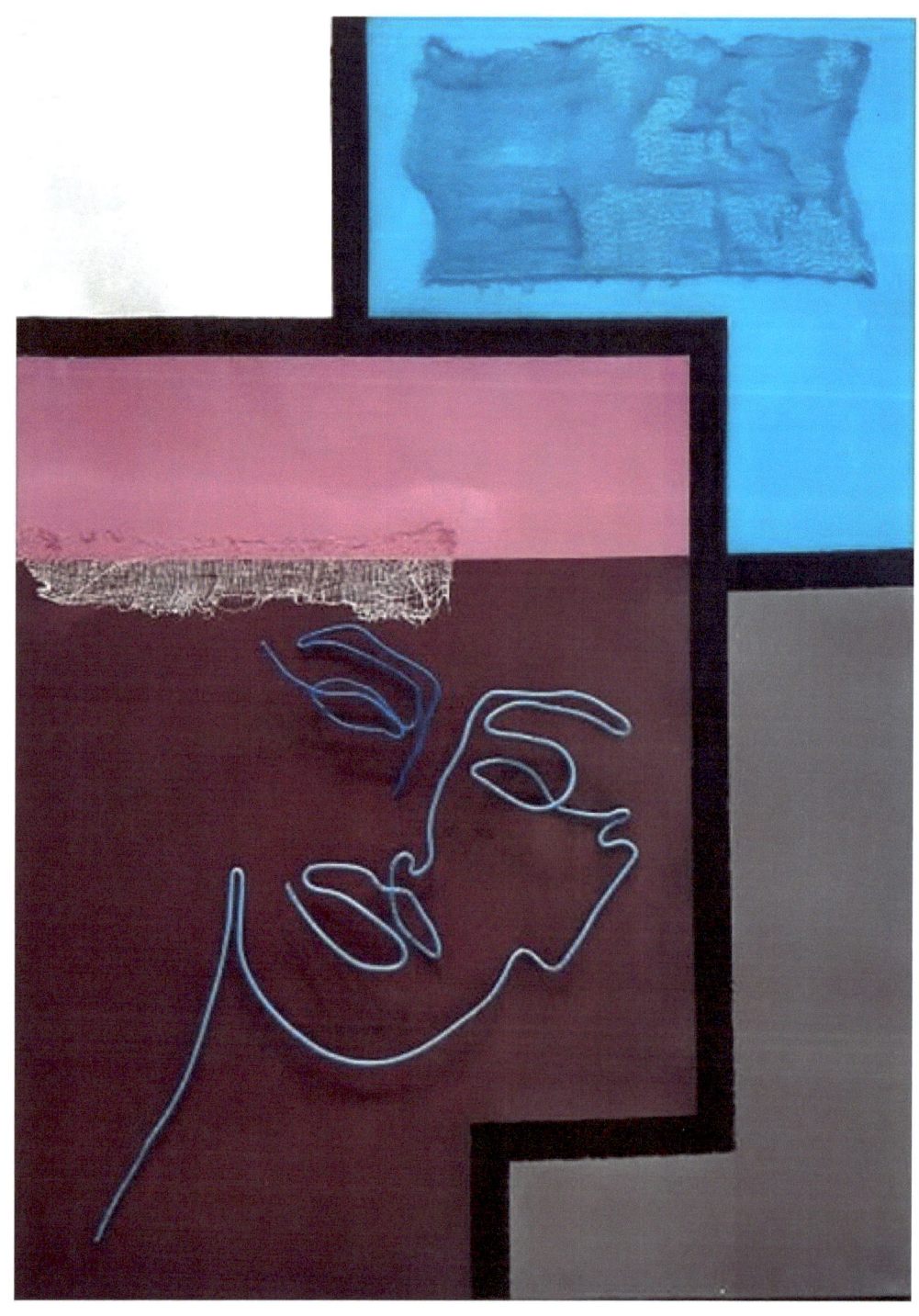

Acrylic and metal thread on canvas, 80 by 60 cm

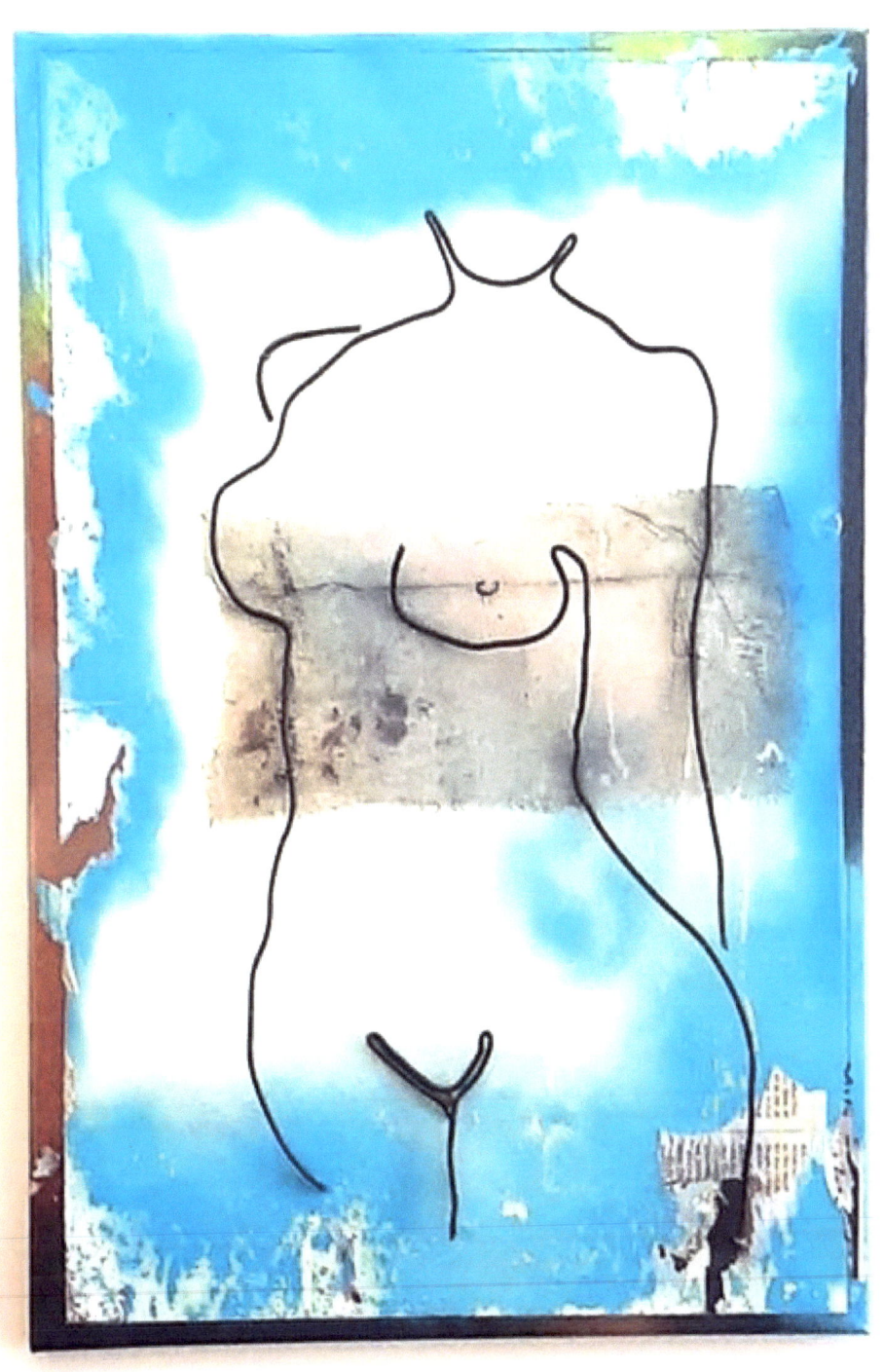

Metal wire and acrylic on canvas, 40 by 30 cm

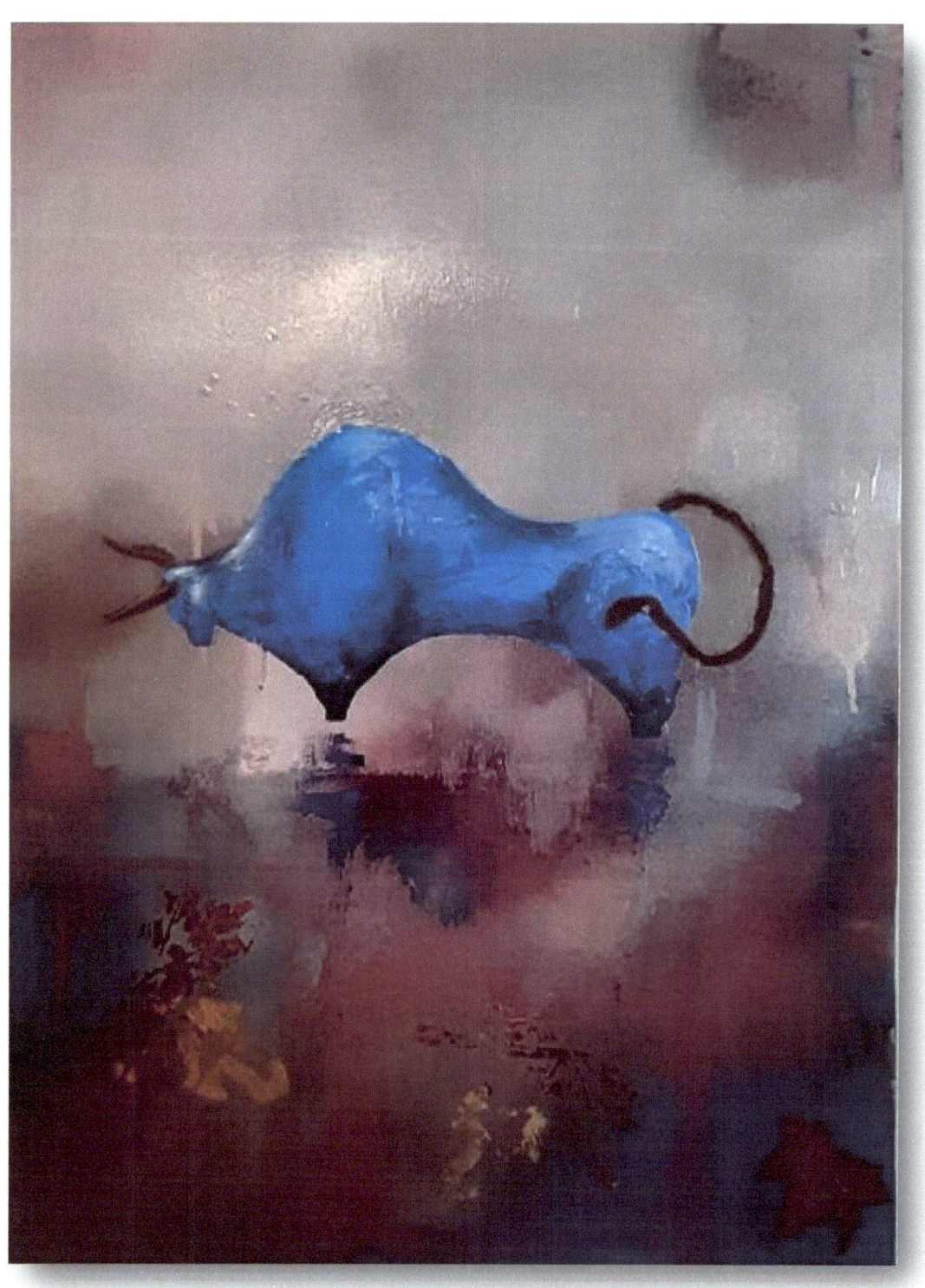

Acrylic on canvas, 68 by 98 cm

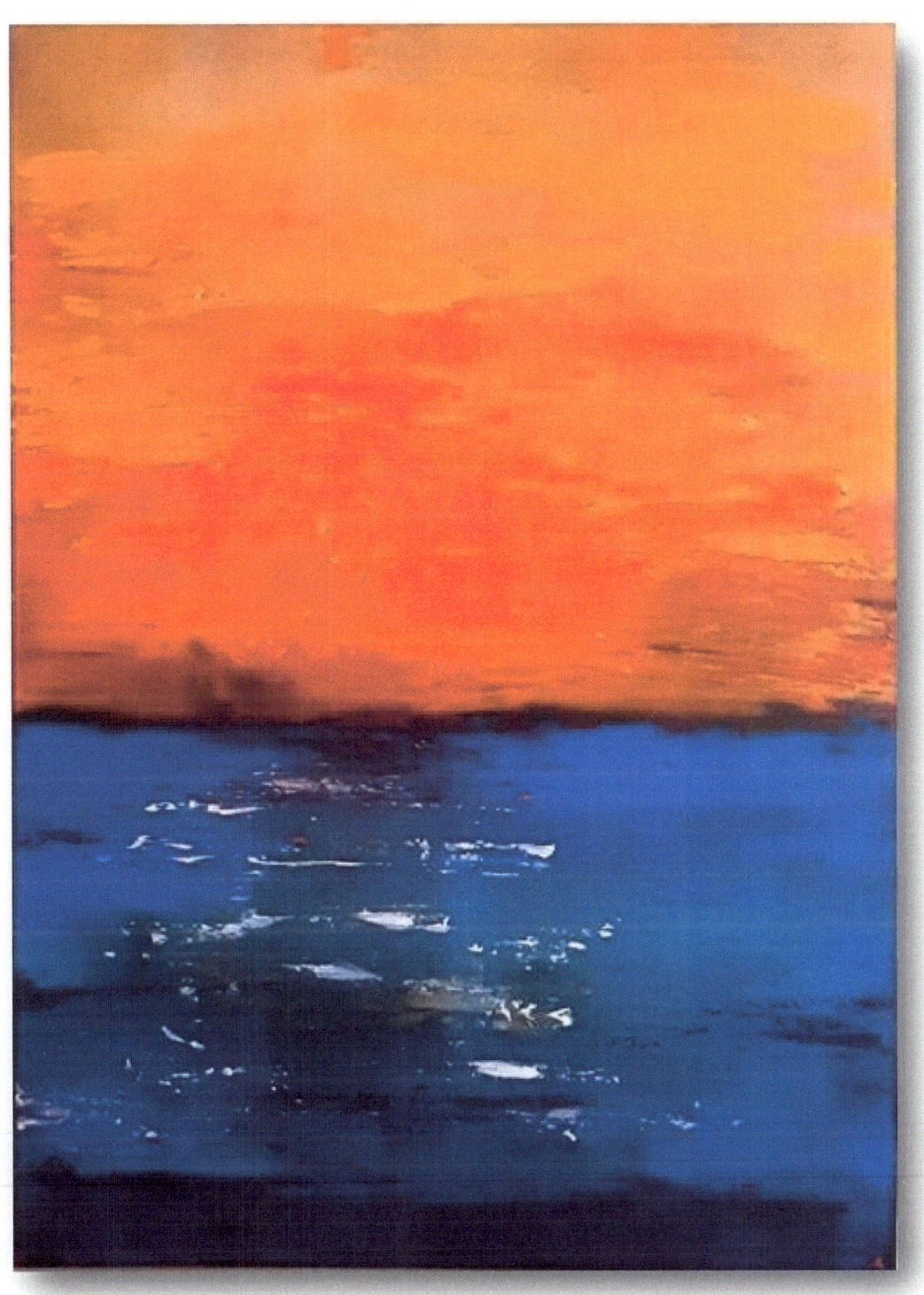

Acrylic on canvas, 68 by 98 cm

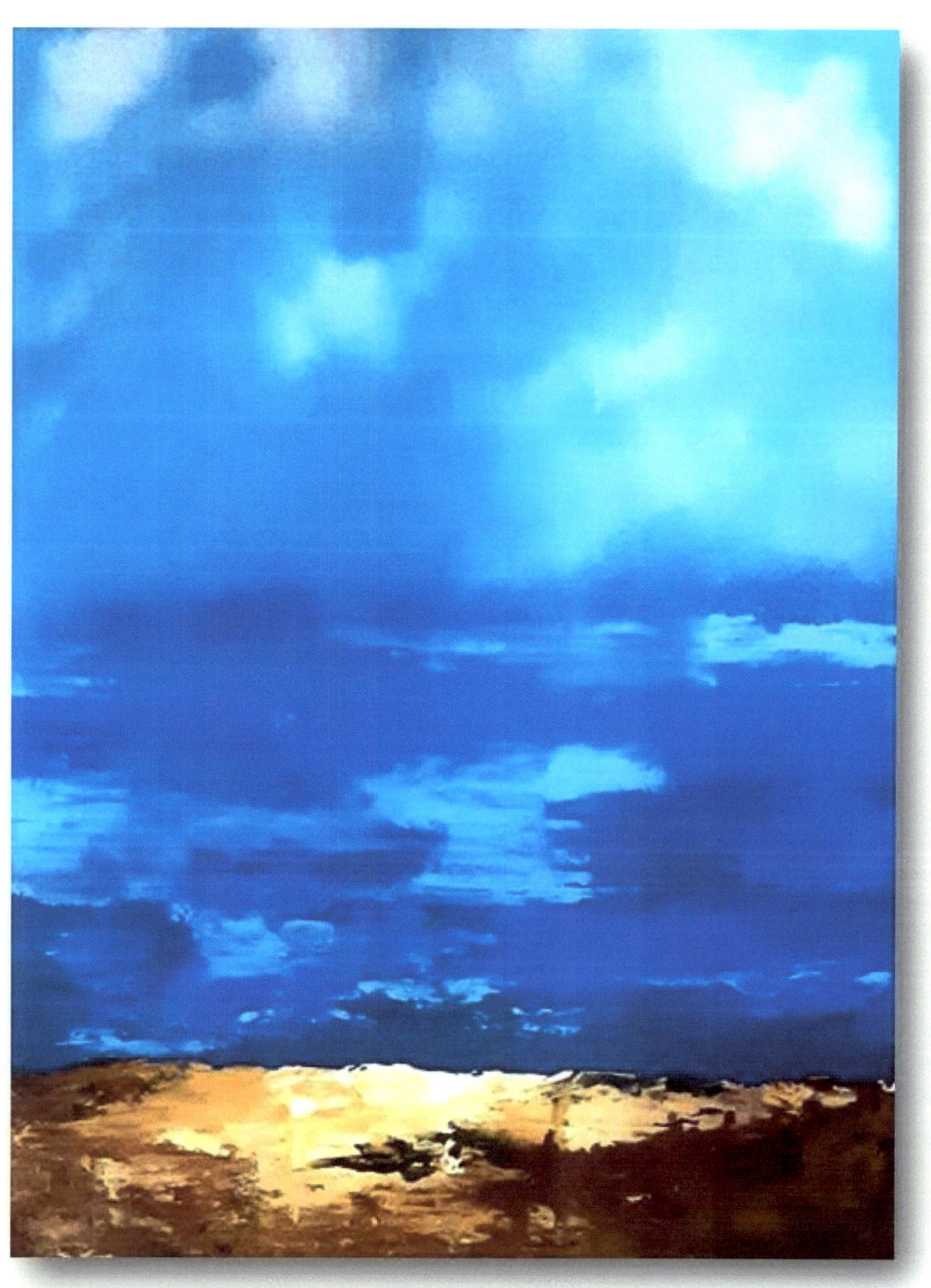

Acrylic on canvas, 68 by 98 cm

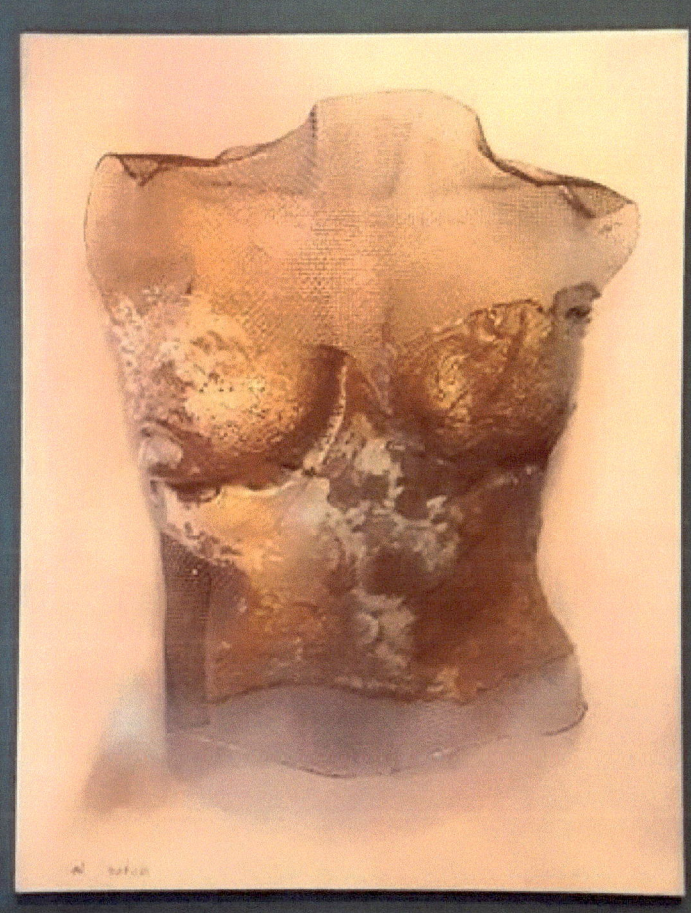

Grid sculpture

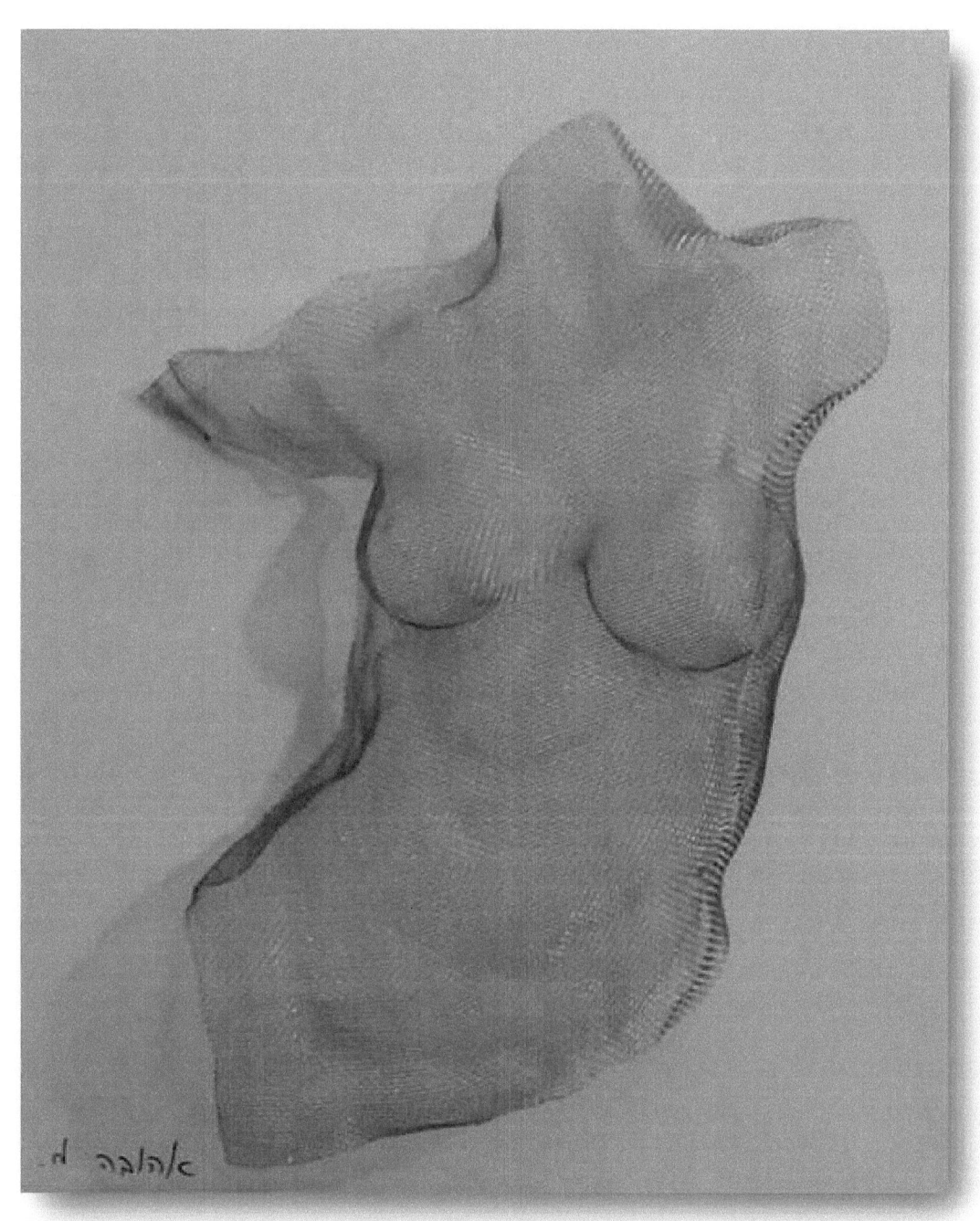

Grid sculpture

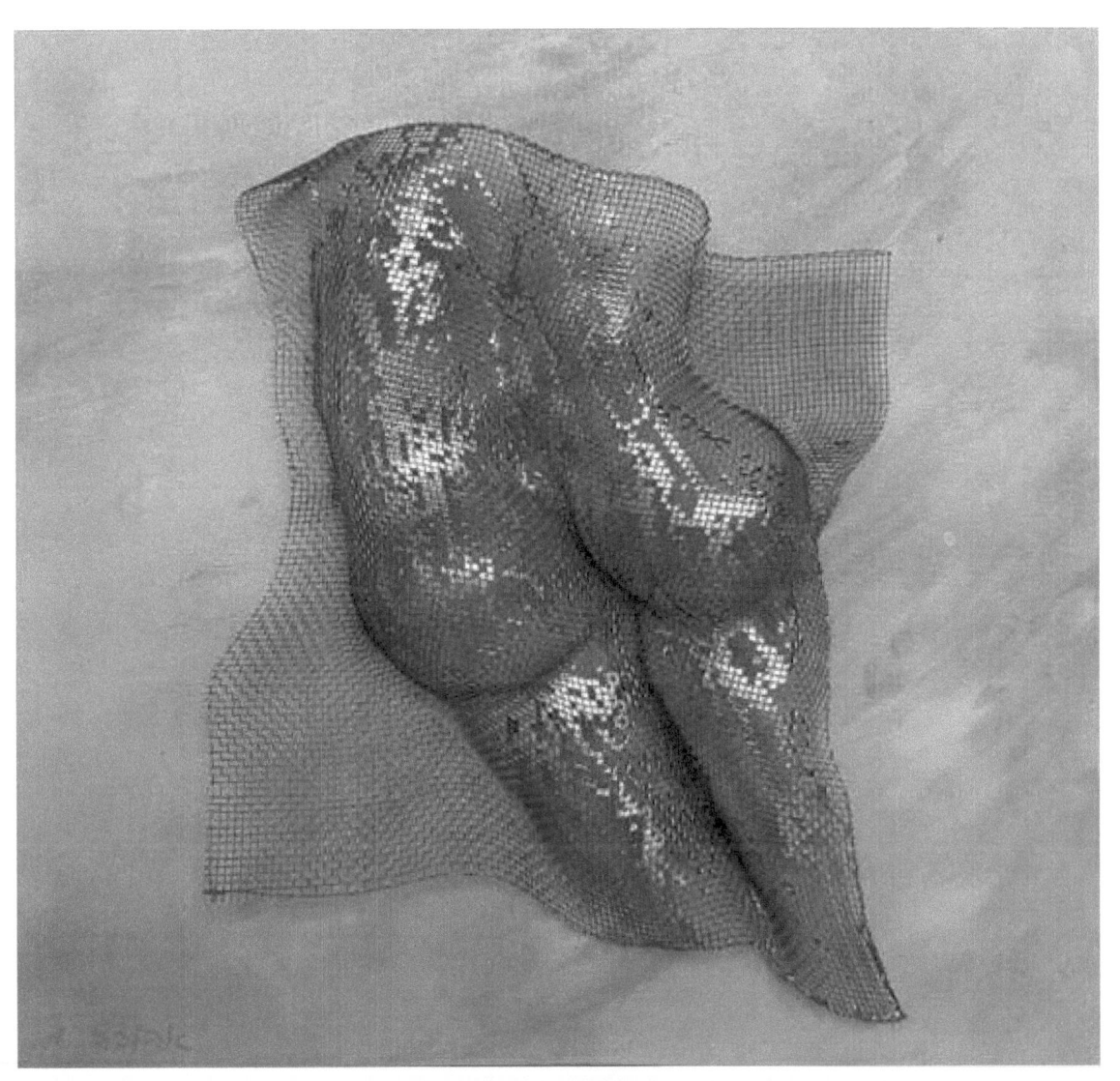

Grid sculpture

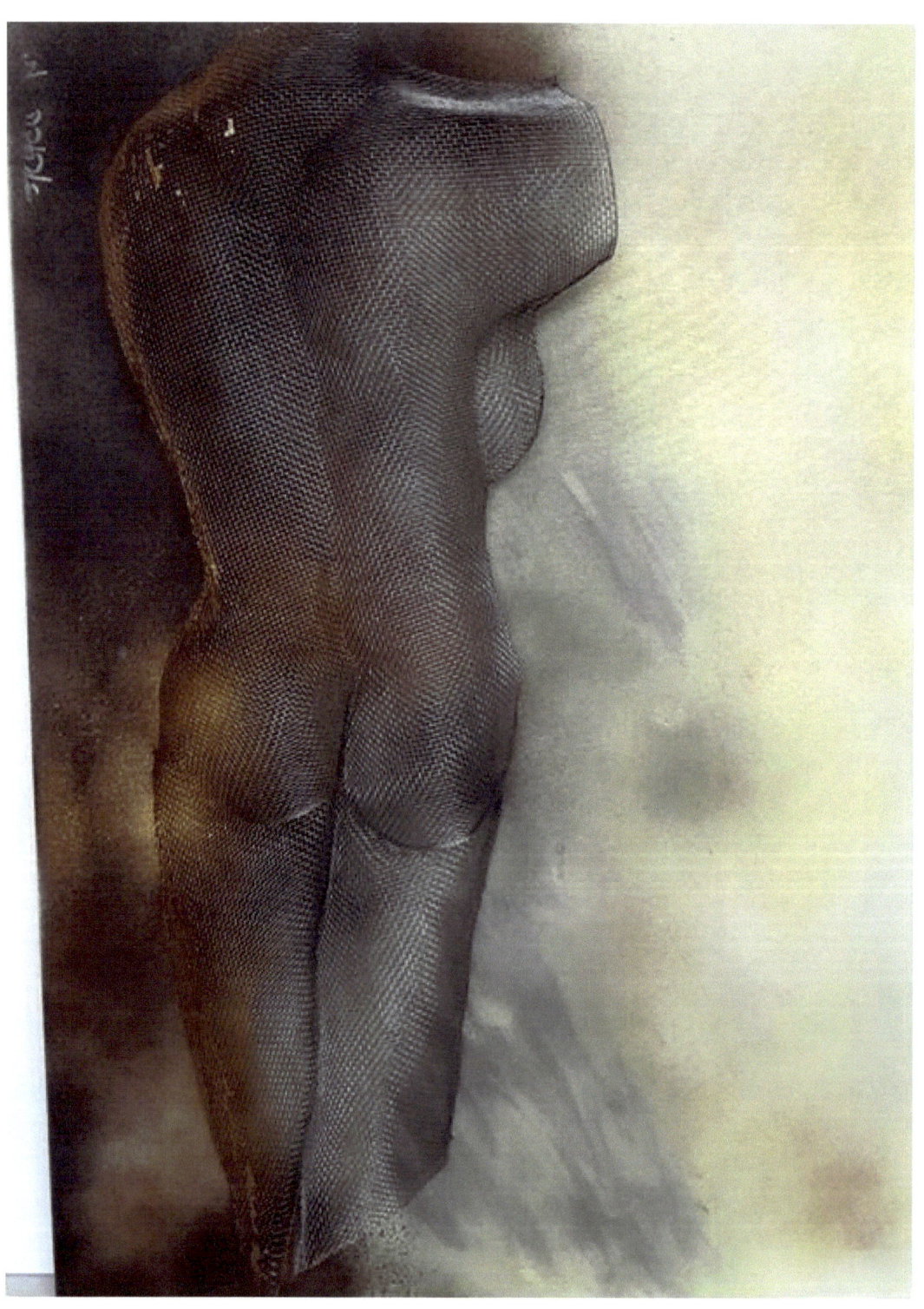

Grid sculpture

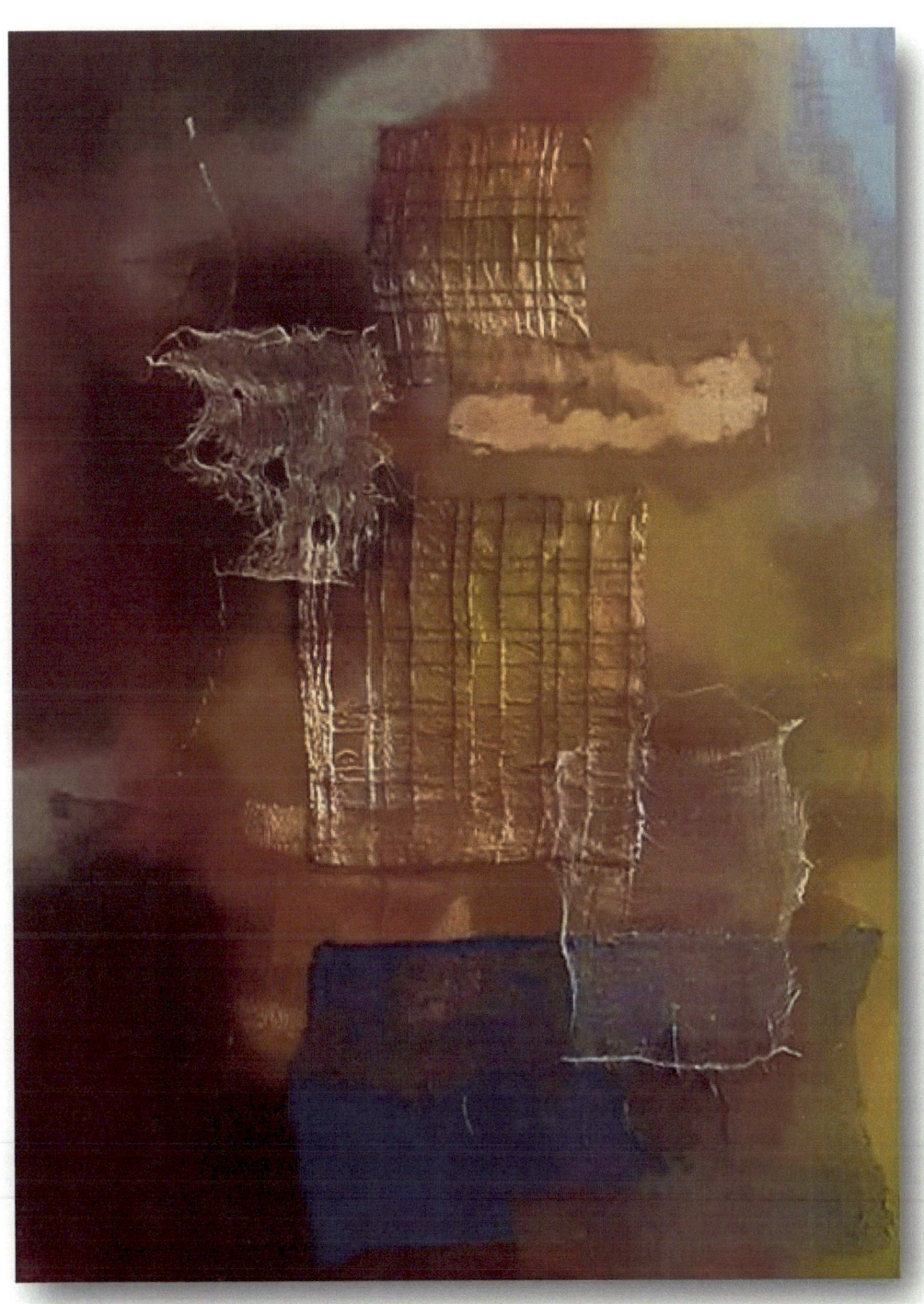

Mixed media on canvas, 68 by 98 cm

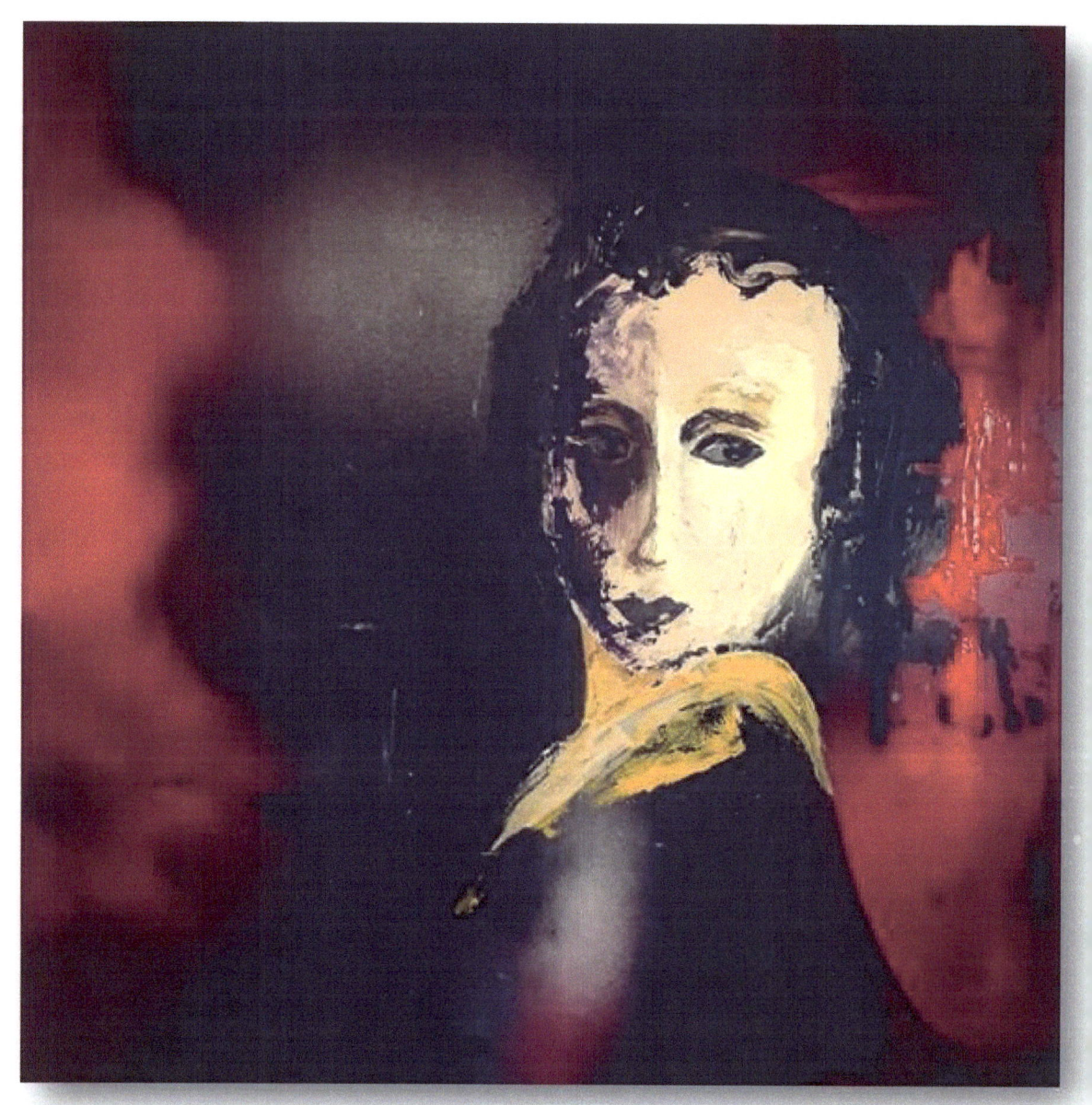

Acrylic on canvas, 80 by 80 cm

www.ingramcontent.com/pod-product-compliance
Lightning Source LLC
Chambersburg PA
CBHW040408220526
45473CB00004B/1170